Gildroy W. Griffin

Studies in Literature

Gildroy W. Griffin

Studies in Literature

ISBN/EAN: 9783337203009

Printed in Europe, USA, Canada, Australia, Japan

Cover: Foto ©Thomas Meinert / pixelio.de

More available books at **www.hansebooks.com**

STUDIES IN LITERATURE

BY

G. W. GRIFFIN

BALTIMORE:
HENRY C. TURNBULL, Jr.
1870.

Entered, according to Act of Congress, in the year 1870, by
HENRY C. TURNBULL, Jr.
In the Clerk's Office of the District Court of the District of Maryland.

TO

VIRGILINE,

OUR SWEETEST JOY AND BRIGHTEST HOPE,

THIS VOLUME

IS

AFFECTIONATELY INSCRIBED.

CONTENTS.

	PAGE
GEORGE D. PRENTICE,	1
VICTOR HUGO,	25
MARMONTEL'S BELISARIUS,	30
VATHEK,	39
THE TEMPEST,	47
THE SCARLET LETTER,	52
EDWIN BOOTH'S MACBETH,	58
PERCY BYSSHE SHELLEY,	69
ANTONY AND CLEOPATRA,	76
CYMBELINE,	83
HAMLET,	89
DAVID GARRICK,	97
THACKERAY,	104
ALL'S WELL THAT ENDS WELL,	119
DREAMING,	117
DANTE,	121
THE GYPSIES,	126
AUTOGRAPHS,	132
JANAUSCHEK,	144
A PHILOLOGICAL STUDY,	152

STUDIES IN LITERATURE.

GEORGE D. PRENTICE.

THE life of this distinguished poet and journalist has been a crown of glory to the world; but only those who have been brought within the charmed circle of his acquaintance, and enjoyed his confidence and friendship, can form the least idea of the peerless grace and lofty beauty of his soul. He seemed to belong to a higher order of beings than those of this earth; and I can but feel, in approaching the subject of his memory, that I am treading upon sacred ground. He was my best and truest friend. I consulted him upon nearly every duty and obligation that I owed to society and to the world, and I always found him the wisest and gentlest teacher, and the safest and surest guide. His heart was so eloquent in the deep pathos and purity of its affections, that I was never in his presence without feeling wiser and better. I had known him so long and well, and had been the recipient of so many acts of love and kindness from his hands, that I began to look upon his existence as necessary for my happiness upon earth. There was nothing that he could do for me that he did not do cheerfully. In no instance did he endeavor to make me sensible of the obligation I owed him, but ever appeared more like the receiver than the giver. There has scarcely been a day during the past five years that I did not see him, or receive some message from him. It was his custom to spend at least two evenings in every week at my house. A chair was placed for him regularly at our table, and no one was allowed to occupy it during his absence. This little mark of respect seemed always to please him exceedingly, for even trivial kindnesses were never passed unnoticed by him, and those who conferred them were always well paid by some pleasant word or acknowledgment. There was a mildness, a dignity, a love and a patience about him that seemed peculiarly his own; and now that he is dead I feel half ashamed of the little that I can add to his memory.

GEORGE DENNISON PRENTICE was born at Griswold, Connecticut, on the 18th of December, 1802. He displayed very early in life talents of no common order. He excited the admiration of every one who knew him by the marvellous facility with which he acquired the most difficult and complicated branches of knowledge. He was able to read fluently when only four years of age. He was a fine Greek and Latin scholar, and at the age of fifteen could translate and parse any sentence in Homer or Virgil. At this time he was prepared to enter the Sophomore class at college, but was compelled to teach a district school in order to defray the expense of a collegiate education. In 1820 he entered Brown University, at Providence,

Rhode Island, where he was graduated in 1823. A few years later he studied law, and was soon admitted to the bar. He did not find the law congenial to his tastes, and he devoted himself to the profession of literature. In 1828 he started the *New-England Review*. This paper was a success from the beginning. The editor at once distinguished himself by his bold and incisive style of writing. In 1830 he left the *New-England Review* in charge of the poet Whittier, and accepted an invitation to go to Kentucky for the purpose of writing the biography of Henry Clay. As soon as he reached Lexington, the home of Mr. Clay, he went to work at once upon the biography. It was completed in a very short time. It met with a most enthusiastic reception, not only from the people of Kentucky, but from the entire Whig party of the nation. It contains by far the most correct account ever given to the public, of the life of that distinguished statesman, as well as the most animated and eloquent exposition of the political principles of his party. Mr. Clay cherished for his biographer the warmest feelings of affection, and often said that he owed the greater part of his fame to him. It is almost useless to speak of the services Mr. PRENTICE rendered Mr. Clay, for they are so manifold and varied that the names of the great statesman and journalist are inseparably associated.

Mr. PRENTICE removed to Louisville in the month of September, 1830, and on the 24th day of the following November he published the first number of the *Louisville Journal*. The politics of the country were at that time exciting in the extreme. The Democratic party determined, if possible, to defeat Mr. Clay in his own State. The leading Democratic organ in Kentucky was a paper called the *Louisville Advertiser*. It was under the editorial management of Shadrack Penn, one of the most eloquent and effective writers in the State. Mr. Penn's friends had the most unbounded confidence in him. They predicted that he would demolish Mr. PRENTICE at a single blow.

Those who remember the warfare waged between these two knights of the quill, have no difficulty in realising that there were giants in those days. Each of the editors was recognised as a champion with whom ordinary mortals must not interfere. In their respective fields of force they possessed powers rarely rivalled. Mr. Penn had a great advantage in a well and widely established reputation in the *venue* where the case was to be tried, while Mr. PRENTICE was comparatively a stranger, and apparently weak. Mr. Penn had rarely met an editor able to cope with him. After he had vanquished the redoubtable Amos Kendall, on the Old and New Court issues which convulsed the State, Mr. Penn was the recognised champion of the party that had triumphed in the great contest in which those issues were tried. In this condition of things, it is not likely that Mr. Penn dreaded any contemporary writer on politics. The comparatively young Connecticut writer had fully surveyed the ground before consenting to link himself with the enterprise of a new daily paper in Louisville. He had measured the powers of the veteran Penn, but he had unbounded confidence in his own powers.

When the *emeute* began to brew in the *Advertiser*, Mr. PRENTICE gave an admonitory warning, announcing that without desiring strife he was ready for it. He stated that his editorial quiver was armed with quills of all sizes, from those of the humming-bird to those of the eagle. The war began, and was waged with activity and vigor for the space of eleven years. Each of the combatants possessed great powers, and up to the end of the war each had hosts of friends. Mr. PRENTICE became famous throughout the Union. The remarkable purity of his diction — a purity in which he had few equals and no superior; his wonderful versatility of expression, by which he was able to use the same thing many times, and never twice alike ; the Attic salt of his wit, the torturing power of his irony, his satire and sarcasm, the terse epigrammatic force which enabled him often to overwhelm an antagonist in a single sentence, made him the most popular and renowned journalist in the country. These qualities made Mr. PRENTICE a power in the land ; a power which he never abused. He was at all times placable, even with those who had most abused him. This is beautifully portrayed in his reconciliation with Mr. Penn. I am indebted to Dr. T. S. Bell, of Louisville, for an account of this noble feature in the lives of the two renowned journalists. Dr. Bell was the intimate friend of each of the editors ; and on the eve of the departure of Mr. Penn for St. Louis, Dr. Bell proposed to both gentlemen the project of an interview. Each assented to the proposal, and each of them gave Dr. Bell full power to act for him. The interview took place at Dr. Bell's office, and commenced and ended most happily. Mr. PRENTICE began by expressing the hope that the necessity of Mr. Penn's departure was not absolute, and begged to know of Mr. Penn whether he, Mr. PRENTICE, could be of any service in aiding him to remain. He eloquently alluded to the long series of Kentucky enterprises, and the numerous recognised schemes for the prosperity of Louisville, that endeared Mr. Penn to the principles of Kentucky, and Mr. PRENTICE deplored the departure of Mr. Penn from the State as a public calamity. Towards the close of the interview, Mr. PRENTICE assured Mr. Penn of his earnest purpose to give him all the aid in his power towards making Mr. Penn's career in Missouri a success. This pledge he fulfilled. It is difficult to conceive of anything more beautiful of its kind than Mr. PRENTICE's tribute to Mr. Penn upon the departure of the latter for St. Louis.

Mr. PRENTICE read the article, before publishing it, to Dr. Bell, as the common friend of Mr. Penn and of himself, and asked for any suggestions for elaborating this magnanimous editorial. I need not add that Mr. Penn was much gratified with it.

Mr. PRENTICE was one of the most industrious men that ever edited a daily paper. He wrote with great facility, but kept himself well posted in all political matters, not only those that were contemporary with him, but with those of the past. Until within a few years he never left the office until the editorial page was imposed as he desired it to be, and locked up in the chase.

In 1840 he was attacked with a disease called *Chorea Scriptorum*, caused by excessive writing. This disease shows itself only when the hand attempts to write. Mr. PRENTICE, could handle other things than a writing instrument without any trouble. Indeed, for a long time after the appearance of the disease, he was able to write many words until the thumb was pressed towards the index finger, when the pen would fly from him as though some one had struck it. One morning while suffering in this way, he composed a beautiful song for his friend, Dr. T. S. Bell. Mr. PRENTICE'S amanuensis was not in, and he stepped over to the Doctor's office, and asked him to write something for him, saying "It is for you and your wife." Mr. PRENTICE then dictated the following beautiful lines, which were afterwards set to music by a distinguished artist of Poland :

> "We've shared each other's smiles and tears
>   Through years of wedded life ;
> And love has bless'd those fleeting years,
>   My own, my cherished wife.
>
> "And if, at times, the storm's dark shroud
>   Has rested in the air,
> Love's beaming sun has kissed the cloud,
>   And left the rainbow there.

"In all our hopes, in all our dreams,
  Love is forever nigh,
A blossom in our path it seems,
  A sunbeam in our sky.

"For all our joys of brightest hue
  Grow brighter in love's smile,
And there's no grief our hearts e'er knew
  That love could not beguile."

Those who were not acquainted with Mr. PRENTICE's forgiving nature, have been surprised that his enemies should so often display a readiness to forget and forgive the many severe things he said about them.

At one time, Mike Walsh, a prominent Democratic politician of New York, provoked a quarrel with him, and was severely punished for his temerity. Mr. PRENTICE handled him without gloves, and let fall a perfect torrent of wit and sarcasm and satire against him. At the time of the controversy Mr. PRENTICE and Mr. Walsh were personally strangers to each other, and as may naturally be supposed the latter did not care to alter the relation. They met, however, some time afterward, at a dinner-party in Washington city. Walsh was a splendid-looking man. He was tall and commanding, and everything about him denoted dignity and elegance of demeanor. As Mr. PRENTICE advanced, Walsh fixed his piercing eyes upon him without offering his hand, and exclaimed: "You are GEORGE D. PRENTICE, are you?" Mr. PRENTICE bowed an assent, and Walsh said: "You must know, sir, that I like you; although you have skinned me from the crown of my head to the soles of my feet, your instrument was so sharp and so skilfully used that the operation was rather pleasant than otherwise."

During Mr. PRENTICE's long and eventful life he was engaged in many controversies, and, strange to say, he invariably came out triumphant. Some of his controversies led to violent personal encounters; but I have his own testimony, and that of many of the oldest and best citizens of Louisville, that he was not the aggressor in a single instance.

Some years ago, George James Trotter, editor of the Kentucky *Gazette*, fired at him on Market street, in Louisville, without the slightest warning, and wounded him near the heart. Mr. PRENTICE, with knife in hand, instantly threw him to the ground, and held him irresistibly in his grasp. A large crowd gathered around the scene, and nearly every one present cried out, "Kill him! kill him!" Mr. PRENTICE instantly let go his hold, and exclaimed: "I cannot kill a disarmed and helpless man!"

Mr. PRENTICE'S forgiving nature was so widely known that those who had wronged him most did not hesitate to accost him in terms of apparent friendship.

On one occasion, Thos. Jefferson Pew, without the slightest provocation, said some very scandalous things about him. Pew was so unworthy of PRENTICE'S notice that I do not believe he ever replied to him; but one morning, several years afterward, he had the audacity to enter PRENTICE'S office. Pew was in a wretched and filthy condition; his clothes were worn and seedy, and with uncombed hair and unshaved face, he presented a most disgusting and loathsome appearance. He called PRENTICE aside, and after some conversation left the office. Fortunatus Cosby, the distinguished poet, was in the room at the time, and asked Mr. PRENTICE the name of his unsightly visitor. Mr. PRENTICE replied: "He is Thos. Jefferson Pew. He told me that he was in distress, and that he wanted two dollars and a half for the purpose of going to see his mother." "Yes," said Cosby, "and I suppose you were silly enough to give it to him?" "No," replied PRENTICE, "I recollected that I had a mother, and asked myself the question what she would have thought of me had I appeared before her in such a filthy condition, and I gave him *twenty-five dollars*, and told him to go to see his mother in the garb of a gentleman."

In 1835 Mr. PRENTICE was married to Miss Harriet Benham, the daughter of Col. Joseph Benham, a distinguished lawyer of Kentucky.

The *Louisville Journal*, under the guidance of Mr. PRENTICE, for a period of thirty years probably exercised more political power and influence than any other paper in America. It has been said, and said truly, that "among the newspaper-press it was a monocrat." It exercised as much influence in the field of literature as in the field of politics. It made and unmade poets and essayists as well as politicians and statesmen. A writer whose contributions appeared in its columns considered his reputation as an author established. Fortunatus Cosby, John J. Piatt, Amelia Welby, Sallie M. Bryan and many others equally distinguished, owe their first public introduction to it.

Its editor became daily more and more popular. He was known almost as well in Europe as in America. He scorned to be subservient to any clique or party. There was no mortgage on his brain. Everything that was mean, or little, or false, or meretricious, was foreign to him. He never courted popular applause. It seemed that there was nothing outside of the range of his genius. No such word as *failure* was written in his lexicon. He accomplished everything he undertook. His learning was varied, thorough, and profound. What he did not know he never affected to possess. He imitated no one. He created models rather than followed them. He had no especial fondness for quotations. Whenever he availed himself of the writings of others, they were so refined in the crucible of his genius that they became his own. His memory was not only retentive, but trustworthy in the fullest sense of the word. His command over language was extraordinary. It was tyrannous. He could think of a thousand words at once, and select the one best suited to his purpose. He was a natural grammarian. I have heard him say that he understood every principle of English grammar as if by intuition, and that when a child he astonished his teacher by finishing the study of Lindley Murray in less than a week. His style of writing was quick, subtle, powerful, and massive. There was nothing dull or commonplace about it. He wrote with marvellous facility, and often dashed off from six to ten columns of printed matter a day. His wit was keen, sparkling, and original. His humor was rich and racy, and like that of Lamb and Fielding, at once broad and fine. He was always willing to fight an up-hill battle, for he was as skilful in attack as in defence. His anger was slow to arouse, but when aroused, it was like the lightning's flash, brief and quick, but sure.

The affluence of Mr. PRENTICE in genius and in equipments of education seemed to be well-nigh endless. He was as generous in the beneficent use of his intellectual wealth as he was great in the magnitude of its possession. Those who knew him intimately during his editorial career in Louisville, can easily call up from the storehouse of memory hundreds of examples of his judicious, unstinted and benevolent kindness to young aspirants for fame. The term judicious kindness is illustrated in the case of that lovely song-bird, Amelia. Many persons who saw her charming poems in the columns of the *Louisville Journal*, and who knew of her limited education, were unable to conceive that she was capable of writing the beautiful poetry that appeared in her name. The surmise was quite common among this class of persons that Mr. PRENTICE either wrote the poems or corrected and dressed them up for her. A distinguished gentleman of Louisville who was quite intimate with Amelia, and had often seen her write her poems, mentioned the current story on one occasion to Mr. PRENTICE, who said: "I recognised the priceless beauty o her genius too well to spoil it in that way. I never correc ted a word in any of her writings. On the few occasions when she had used a word which I would not have used, I sent her manuscript back to her with the defective word marked, and she immediately corrected the diction herself. Beyond that I never aided, nor had occasion to aid her."

Amelia loved music, and played instrumental music beautifully without any education in it. She sang as sweetly, and as melodiously, as she wrote. She had an intense love for flowers, and possessed a husband whose gifts as a floriculturist gave him power to abundantly gratify her floral desires. Some of her beautiful tributes to music, birds, and flowers, adorn the tasteful column erected to her memory in Cavehill cemetery.

Nothing in the career of Mr. PRENTICE was more astonishing than the ease and naturalness with which he at all times called his gifts of education into duty, when an occasion called for their exercise. He never used Greek or Latin words in his compositions, yet such was his intimacy with those languages that upon the spur of the moment he often gave criticisms of as profound a character as though he devoted himself exclusively to the study of the classics. Dr. Bell was his physician for thirty-seven years, and was one of his most intimate friends through that long period, yet he was not even aware that Mr. PRENTICE was almost a perfect master of mathematics until Dr. S. G. Howe, the renowned philanthropist, visited Kentucky at the invitation of a number of her citizens, to aid in the establishment of a State institution for the education of the blind. Dr. Howe brought with him a pupil of the "Perkins Institute for the Blind," and a pupil also of Harvard College. This pupil, Mr. Smith, possessed a remarkable education as a musician, classical scholar, linguist, and mathematician. Dr. Howe, who was a student of Brown University with Mr. PRENTICE, requested Mr. PRENTICE to attend the public meeting of the citizens of Louisville where Mr. Smith was to show that blindness was not a barrier to the acquisition of a varied and extensive and profound education. Mr. PRENTICE was called upon at the meeting to make important problems for solution by Mr. Smith. The first problems were not remarkably recondite, but as soon as Mr. PRENTICE discovered Mr. Smith's proficiency, he rose into the highest departments of mathematics, and made problems that might have found an appropriate place in Hutton's Mathematical Recreations, which could not be called recreations to any one but a profound mathematician.

In 1860 Mr. PRENTICE published a volume of his witticisms under the title of "Prenticeana." This book consists principally of paragraphs from the *Louisville Journal*, and a few written for the *New York Ledger*. Mr. PRENTICE had for years been repeatedly solicited to allow the publication of such a volume, but uniformly declined because there were serious objections to many of his wittiest paragraphs on account of partisan bitterness expressed in them. He finally consented to publish the book, from a knowledge of the fact that if he did not collect his own paragraphs others would, and make the selection with far less regard to the feelings of many who were his friends.

Prenticeana contains about three hundred pages. There is not a single paragraph in it that is not characterised by the most piercing keenness and the most exquisite aptness. It does not, however, contain by any means the best specimens of PRENTICE's wit and humor, but there is probably no similar collection in any language that will begin to compare with it.

At the beginning of the late war Mr. PRENTICE espoused the cause of the Union. He put on his armor and went to work in earnest. He infused into the columns of his paper all the ardor and enthusiasm of his nature. His old friends, many of whom had periled their lives for him, remonstrated with him, warned him, and threatened him. Even his two sons, whom he loved with a devotion almost unequalled, had entered the Southern army to battle for what they deemed a sacred duty; but undaunted, he called the people to arms and to consolidate a mighty phalanx against an unrighteous rebellion. He did more. He used all the power and eloquence of his genius to persuade the Southern people to put an end to hostilities and to pursue a hopeless struggle no longer.

I need not dwell further upon this theme. The part he enacted has passed into history. Had he adopted a different course, the most fearful consequences to the Government might have been the result.

In person Mr. PRENTICE was above the medium height. His head was finely shaped; his figure was erect, but his exceedingly sloping shoulders gave him rather a drooping appearance. He was dignified and elegant in his bearing, and graceful and natural in all his movements and actions. His hands and feet were unusually small; his face was round and full; his features were irregular but not homely. His forehead was broad and high, and awed the beholder by its expression of intellectual vigor. His eyes were his finest feature; they were of a dark brown color, rather small, but lustrous and full of strange intelligence —

"Deep searching seen, and seeing from afar."

His voice was low-toned and persuasive, but, free as a fountain, it took the form of the conduit thought.

He was one of the finest conversationists I ever heard. He illumined every subject upon which he touched. He knew exactly when to begin and when to stop. He had no set speeches. He delivered no monologues. He never wearied his listeners or insulted them by presuming upon their ignorance. His favorite poets were Virgil, Byron, and Shelley. He placed Virgil even above Homer. He said there was a freshness, a naturalness and a stately grandeur about the verses of Virgil that were unequalled. He talked more of Shelley than of Byron, and I believe saw more to love and admire in him both as a man and a poet. Mr. PRENTICE, I believe, thought more of Rousseau than of any other French author. He once asked me to read the *Nouvelles Heloise:* "but for heaven's sake," said he, "read it in the original text. There is a *fineness* about Rousseau that cannot be translated."

Mr. PRENTICE'S favorite German author was Jean Paul Richter. Had read everything from his pen. I heard him once advise a young writer to adopt Richter's style as a model, "that is," said he, "if you must have a model."

Mr. PRENTICE was one of the best judges of character I ever knew. It was almost impossible to hide truth from him. He could see at a glance through the most guarded meanness and hypocrisy. He never doubted the constancy of a friend. Whenever he formed an attachment, it was almost sure to last through life. There was not a particle of selfishness in his nature. He was kind and gentle and charitable to a fault, and felt no enmity towards his rivals. He never allowed his political feelings to alter his personal relations. I have often heard him speak in the kindest and most affectionate terms of Mr. Greeley. These two great journalists were for many years the most bitter political opponents, and although engaged in a countless number of polemic duels, neither of them at any time entertained the slightest doubt of the honesty and sincerity of the other's convictions. When Mr. Greeley came to Louisville for the purpose of delivering one of his famous lectures, Mr. PRENTICE urged me to go to hear him, saying, " I regard him as the ablest as well as the most conscientious journalist in the North; he has outlived the ordinary period of life, but his mind is in the fullness of its power. It is something for the people of the rising generation to look upon the form and features of such a brave and daring chieftain. When he shall depart from among us he will probably not leave a single peer behind."

On the evening of Mr. Greeley's lecture Mr. PRENTICE occupied a chair near the speaker's stand, and listened attentively to every word that fell from his lips. A few weeks after the lecture Mr. PRENTICE wrote the following beautiful poem to him, entitled " To a Political Opponent " : —

"I send thee, Greeley, words of cheer,
　Thou bravest, truest, best of men;
For I have marked thy strong career,
　As traced by thy own sturdy pen.
I've seen thy struggles with the foes
　That dared thee to the desperate fight,
And loved to watch thy goodly blows,
　Dealt for the cause thou deem'st the right.

" Thou'st dared to stand against the wrong
　When many faltered by thy side;
In thy own strength hast dared be strong,
　Nor on another's arm relied.
Thy own bold thoughts thou'st dared to think,
　Thy own great purposes avowed;
And none have ever seen thee shrink
　From the fierce surges of the crowd.

" Thou, all unaided and alone,
　Didst take thy way in life's young years,
With no kind hand clasped in thy own,
　No gentle voice to soothe thy tears.

> But thy high heart no power could tame,
>   And thou hast never ceased to feel
> Within thy veins a sacred flame
>   That turned thy iron nerves to steel.
>
> "I know that thou art not exempt
>   From all the weaknesses of earth;
> For passion comes to rouse and tempt
>   The truest souls of mortal birth.
> But thou hast well fulfilled thy trust,
>   In spite of love and hope and fear;
> And e'en the tempest's thunder-gust
>   But clears thy spirit's atmosphere.
>
> "Thou still art in thy manhood's prime,
>   Still foremost 'mid thy fellow-men,
> Though in each year of all thy time
>   Thou hast compressed threescore and ten.
> Oh, may each blessed sympathy,
>   Breathed on thee with a tear and sigh,
> A sweet flower in thy pathway be,
>   A bright star in thy clear blue sky."

I regret that the limits prescribed for this article will not admit of an extended notice of Mr. PRENTICE's poetry. It has been said that "he wrote verses simply as a recreation," and that "he estimated lightly his poetic gift." There is no truth whatever in such a conclusion. A more silly thought never took possession of a critic's brain.

Mr. PRENTICE wrote poetry because he loved it, because he could not help it, and because it was one of the elements in which he lived, and moved, and breathed, and had his being. It was so deeply interwoven in his nature that it became an integral part of it, and ever clung around and about him as the tendrils of the ivy to the oak. It was to his existence what the dew and sunshine are to the flowers.

In the stillness of night, when alone in his room, "a time for memory and tears," his great soul loved to commune with itself and the spirit of the universe. I have heard him say that at such moments, if it had not been for his paralysed hand, he could have expressed thoughts such as only the truly inspired feel.

His poems entitled "My Mother's Grave," and a little poem called "Violets" (published in the *Ledger* a few weeks before his death, but written last summer), "The Closing Year," "The Stars," "To a Poetess on her Birth-day," "The River in the Mammoth Cave," are among his best pieces.

The last poem he ever wrote was inscribed to my wife. It is so very beautiful that I hope I shall be pardoned for inserting it here.

"TO MY POETESS—A. M. G.

"Dear Alice, for two happy hours
   I've sat within this little nook,
To muse upon the sweet soul-flowers
   That blossom in thy gentle book.
They lift their white and spotless bells,
   Untouched by frost, unchanged by time;
For they are blessed immortelles
   Transplanted from the Eden clime.

"With pure and deep idolatry
   Upon each lovely page I've dwelt,
Till to thy spirit's sorcery
   My spirit has with reverence knelt.
Oh, every thought of thine to me
   Is like a fount, a bird, a star,
A tone of holy minstrelsy
   Down floating from the clouds afar!

"The fairies have around thee traced
   A circle bright, a magic sphere,
The home of genius, beauty, taste,
   The joyous smile, the tender tear.
   Within that circle, calm and clear,

With Nature's softest dews impearled,
  I sit and list with pitying ear
The tumults of the far-off world.

"Thy book is shut—its flowers remain,
  'Mid this mysterious twilight gloom,
Deep-imaged on my heart and brain,
  And shed their fragrance through my room.
  Ah, how I love their holy bloom,
As in these moonbeams, dim and wan,
  They seem pale blossoms o'er a tomb
That's closed upon the loved and gone!

" Young angel of my waning years,
  Consoler of life's stormiest day,
Magician of my hopes and fears,
  Guide of my dark and troubled way,
To thee this little votive lay
  In gratitude I dedicate,
And with an earnest spirit pray
God's blessing on thy mortal state."

"The Closing Year" is one of his earliest productions. It is more frequently quoted than any of his poems. It is generally regarded as his finest creation. It bears some resemblance to Bryant's "Thanotopsis," to which it has often been compared, but the imagery in "The Closing Year" is far bolder and more inspiring, and besides there is a greater breadth of vision and a wider range of imagination in it. There is, however, in "Thanatopsis" a soft and mellow beauty which is hardly equalled in the other, but there is a compactness, or rather completeness about Bryant's poem that seems to leave no room for suggestiveness.

"The Closing Year," however, is no more beautiful or suggestive than some of Mr. PRENTICE's later productions: for instance, "The Summit of the Sierra Madre," and the "Thoughts on the Far Past," written but a few months before his death.

The truth is, Mr. PRENTICE's genius shone out with increasing splendor toward the close of his life.

In the spring of 1868 he said to me, "I have promised Mr. Bonner to write ten pieces of poetry for the *Ledger*. I am glad of it. I am growing old; pain and sickness and trouble and sorrow have laid their corroding fingers upon my brow, and many think that I cannot write as well as I did in my younger years. I am determined to prove to the contrary, for the rose of my spirit is as bright and fresh as in the days of my boyhood." On the first day of 1869 he said, "The past year was a bad old year; I am glad that it is gone, and that a new one has come with its buds of hope and promise. I am determined to make this year the best year of my life."

How well he fulfilled his resolution is known to the world. There was not a line that fell from his pen that did not bear upon it the ineffaceable stamp of his genius.

I have already referred to the affection in the hands of Mr. PRENTICE. It is called *Chorea Scriptorum*, or *Scriveners, Cramp*. As everything about Mr. PRENTICE is interesting, and in relation to this malady may be instructive, I purpose to give some details additional to those I have mentioned. This *Chorea Scriptorum* was the torture of Mr. PRENTICE's life for over thirty years. It showed itself soon after an exciting canvass for the Presidency, during which he wrote excessively. After trying a multitude of remedies, including galvanism and electricity, without getting relief, he managed to write by using a pen the handle of which was made very large by wrapping silk around it. The pen was grasped by all the fingers and the thumb kept in a state of extension. This plan soon began to fail, and in view of this possibility Mr. PRENTICE learned to write with his left hand. The left hand soon fell into the condition of the right one. Amanuenses were then employed, and upon these he was mainly dependent the rest of his life. The inventive genius of the country was taxed for the invention of a suitable writing-machine for him, but all machines failed, and were of course abandoned. One season he went to New Orleans and placed himself under hydropathic treatment, with a hope of cure. He pursued this until his constitution was severely ravaged. The entire skin was in a state of serious paralysis. This induced him to moderate his use of hydropathy, but he never gave it up until a foreigner whom he had brought with him from New Orleans, and who resided with him because of his great pretensions as a hydropathist, undertook one night to reduce a dislocation of the right shoulder by pouring pitchers of cold water over the shoulder. This filled the cup of Mr. PRENTICE's suspicions of the ignorance of his hydropathic attendant. The family physician was sent for, and he immediately reduced the dislocation. From this time Mr. PRENTICE gave up hydropathy.

This mysterious disease is incurable as a general rule. Neimeyer quotes Fritz for the most sensible view of this malady that has been given. Brown-Sequard and Claude Bernard have explained the phenomena of reflex actions of the nervous system, and have shown that they have their origin mainly in the skin. Fritz says that this affection is a reflex neurosis, in which, however, excitement of the mater nerves is not derived from the cutaneous nerves, as in most reflex neuroses, but proceeds from the muscular nerves. The evil, no matter how long it may be quiescent by abstinence from the use of the muscles that produced the disorder, will invariably show itself even if the hand merely is held in the position for the use that created the malady. As soon as this special use is suspended, the malady ceases during abstinence from this use. Mr. PRENTICE, notwithstanding his afflictions, occasionally wrote poems and letters to his particular friends. Mr. PRENTICE never wearied talking of the beauties and mysteries of nature;

and I have often listened spell-bound, as it were, to his description of the Mammoth Cave with its deep chasms, Stygian pools, awful aisles, fathomless gulfs, crystal fountains, and high-pillared domes fretted with the semblance of stars and flowers. He had arranged with my family to visit the cave during the coming spring. He said, "I want to stand once more upon the banks of Echo River, that wild and wizard stream, in which no star or rainbow ever glassed their image of love and beauty, and extinguish my lamp and see what darkness is."

Mr. PRENTICE, at one time, thought of retiring from the press for the purpose of devoting himself wholly to the pursuit of poetry and other light literature. His son, Col. Clarence G. Prentice, had purchased a beautiful farm nine miles below Louisville, on the Ohio River, and it was his wish that his father should pass the remainder of his life away from the noise and bustle of the city ; but a fondness for newspapers prevented Mr. PRENTICE from acceding to the wishes of his son, and it may be said that he died literally in harness, with accumulated and accumulating duties around him. The last time I saw Mr. PRENTICE in Louisville was the day before he started to his son's. He came to spend the evening with us, and as he sat in his chair in the library I thought that I had never seen him look so well before. He was unusually cheerful, and talked with much pleasure of a visit to his son's during the approaching holidays ; but I fancied that his voice assumed a more melancholy tone than usual when he said, "It is a dreary trip at best during the winter. The roads are in a bad condition, and I look forward to the time with no little anxiety when I shall again have the pleasure of passing an evening with you and Alice and dear little Virgiline." I did not then think that he was soon destined to leave us forever, and that the walls of our little library had echoed for the last time the musical tones of his much-loved voice. The next morning he started to his son's. The day was the coldest of the year. He made the trip in an open carriage. The exposure gave him a severe cold, which resulted in an attack of pneumonia. Dr. J. W. Benson, of Louisville, was sent for, and though he treated Mr. PRENTICE'S disease with the utmost skill, there was not enough strength in his enfeebled constitution to rally from its effects.

I saw Mr. PRENTICE several times during his illness, and each time thought he would recover, but I believe that from the first he anticipated his own destiny. He said, "It is almost impossible for one who has suffered as much as I have to get well; but I do not complain. Death has no terrors for me: this world is not our only home; there is a brighter and a nobler existence beyond the grave."

About a week after the interview I saw him again. He appeared to suffer less pain than at any time during his illness. He inquired kindly, very kindly, about some of his friends in Louisville, and expressed a faint hope that he would be able to go to see them in a few weeks; but I could see in his countenance that he was calmly and patiently awaiting the hour when he would no longer be a dweller beneath the skies. On Friday, the 21st of January, he sent me word that he was dying. I felt it my duty to be by his bed-side. The river had overflowed its banks and the messenger who arrived from the farm reported the roads in an almost impassable condition. My wife, who had loved and admired Mr. PRENTICE'S poetry from her childhood, could not be dissuaded from accompanying me.

We left the city late in the evening, and after proceeding some distance we were compelled to leave the road and go through a dense wood in order to avoid the back water. The darkness was enough to appal stouter hearts than ours. At last we reached a temporary lake which had surrounded the house of the dying.

A little boat was in waiting to take us across the water; but I shall not attempt to describe the picture that presented itself to our view as I lifted my wife into the boat, and saw the physician standing on the steps with a flickering lamp in his hand, reflecting the scene of death in the background.

It was about ten o'clock when we entered the room. Mr. PRENTICE had been in a dying condition since eight in the morning. Not a murmur or word of complaint crossed his lips. My wife approached his bed and said, "Do you know me, Mr. PRENTICE?" He did not recognise her at first, and thinking she was Mrs. Prentice's little sister, Josephine, said, "Yes, it is Josephine;" but when my wife told him her name, he said, "Yes, yes, I know you now; it is Alice."

Mr. PRENTICE was in the full possession of his faculties until the last moment of existence; and I have been informed by Captain J. M. Hewet, who faithfully nursed him throughout his sickness, that in not a single instance did he abandon that patient forbearance and elegant politeness which so beautifully characterised all his actions in life. I have heard it said that the last words of great men are great like themselves, and I felt no little curiosity to hear the last words of Mr. PRENTICE. My wife, who held his hand in hers at the time, says they were (as near as she could understand them), "I want to go, I want to go." I have often stood by the side of the dying, but I never before beheld a death-scene half so solemn or impressive. Mr. PRENTICE's little grandson, Georgie, was asleep on a lounge in the room, unconscious of the end that was awaiting the being he most loved upon earth. The attending physician had ceased to hope even against hope, and weary with watching, fell asleep in his chair. At last Col. Prentice knelt at the side of his father and exclaimed in accents of deepest woe, "Pa, Pa, speak to me once more;" but no answering word came to relieve the awful silence; and a few moments afterwards the golden bowl was broken and the silver cord unstrung, and the spirit of the great man winged its flight to the bosom of the God who gave it.

Victor Hugo.

with a glance at his works.

Victor Hugo has been successful in every department of literature. He has made a brilliant reputation, not only as an essayist and novelist, but as a poet and dramatist. His "Claude Gueux," "Studies upon Mirabeau," and "Littérature et Philosophie Melées," aided in securing his election to the French Academy. His "Marion de Lorme" and "Lucrèce Borgia," in spite of their faults and inconsistencies, and questionable morality, occupy a prominent place upon the stage. His political speeches and orations are read and studied in every civilised country upon the globe. He has written any number of odes and ballads, and lyrical and legendary poems.

He claims to belong to one of the noblest families of France. He traces his noble descent as far back as the year 1531. His residence, "Hauteville House," in the island of Guernsey, is famed for its costly magnificence and sumptuous splendor. There is not a room in it that is not ornamented with some exquisite carvings and rare curiosities. Every department is arranged entirely after his own taste and designs. He has spent a large portion of his life in collecting the rarest works of art, including oak carvings of the middle ages and Renaissance, ancient tapestries, statues, vases, porcelains and enamels. He is said to have covered his walls and furniture with inscriptions and devices illustrative of the most eventful passages in his life and of his peculiar ideas of moral and ethical philosophy.

His chimney-piece is thus described by Lecanu:

Let us imagine a cathedral of carved wood, which, firmly rooted in the flooring, rises in a towering mass to the ceiling, indenting the tapestry above with its highest pinnacles. The doorway is represented by the hearth, and the rose window by a convex mirror placed above the fireplace. The central gable rises in a double entablature, decorated with arcades and fantastic foliage in a deliciously bastard style, in which the *rococo* blends with Byzantine architecture. Surmounted on this are two towers, supported by buttresses, which most happily repeat the ornamentation of the main body. This crowning piece reminds one of the façades of the guild-halls in Antwerp and Bruges. Here, also, as in the roofs of these old remains of the time of Philip II. some plain figures stand out in rigid simplicity, and give life to the bold indental lines of the architecture. One figure is that of a bishop, with a gilt crozier; and on two adjacent escutcheons is the proverb:

CROSSE DE BOIS, EVEQUE D'OR.
CROSSE D'OR, EVEQUE DE BOIS.

Below are two carved figures, representing one, St. Paul, with

LE LIVRE

underneath; the other a monk, and the words

LE CIEL.

On two plain volutes are inscribed the names of the greatest benefactors of humanity, in chronological order:

MOISE, SOCRETE, CHRIST, COLOMB, LUTHER, DANTE, SHAKSPEARE, MOLIERE.

In this palatial residence he indites his literary works for the edification and corruption of mankind. It is here that he stigmatised the execution of John Brown as "worse than the murder of Abel by Cain," and said, "C'est Washington tuant Spartacus." It is here that he wrote "The

Man who Laughs," one of the most singular and meretricious of all his works.

This book is terribly open to criticism, but on that account it is only the more read and praised.

We do not see how it can be regarded in any other light than an attack upon society, upon virtue and religion. It depicts glowingly almost every species of villainy. It is full of hate, revenge, cruelty, murder, intrigue, scandal, animal passion and illicit love. There is scarcely a touch of refinement and purity in it. All the characters, with the exception of Dea, are intensely coarse and vulgar.

The author has grouped together some of the most miserable and contemptible gossip of history. He stops in the midst of a description of his heroine, Josiane, a singular compound of beauty, lasciviousness and bestial passion, to tell us that " Elizabeth is a type that has ruled in England for three centuries. * * She struck with her fist her maids of honor, sent Dudley to the devil, beat Chancellor Burleigh, who whimpered (the old fool), spit upon Matthew, throttled Hatton, boxed Essex on the ears, showed her thigh to Bassompierre. What she did for Bassompierre the Queen of Sheba had done for Solomon. Wherefore it was correct, holy scriptures having established the precedent."

He then goes on to say that Mary Stuart had her weakness for a Rizzio; Maria Theresa had a little familiarity with a negro: whence the Black Abbess. He then indulges in the following amusing contradictions about Josiane: "Never a passion had approached her, and she had gone to the bottom of them all. She had a distaste for realisation and a liking for them at the same time." "It is tiresome to be forced to marry Lord David when there is nothing that I should like better than to love him."

"Josiane, c'était la chair. Rien de plus magnifique. Elle était très-grande, trop grande. Ses cheveux étaient de cette nuance qu'on pourrait nommer le blond pourpre. Elle était grasse, fraîche, robuste, vermeille, avec énormément d'audace et d'esprit. Elle avait les yeux trop intelligibles. D'amant, point ; de chasteté, pas d'avantage. Elle se mûrait dans l'orgueil. Les hommes, fi donc ! un dieu tout au plus était digne d'elle, ou un monstre. Si la vertu consiste dans l'escarpement, Josiane était toute la vertu possible, sans aucune innocence. Elle n'avait pas d'aventures, par dédain ; mais on ne l'eût point fâchée de lui en supposer, pourvu qu'elles fussent étranges et proportionnées à une personne faite comme elle. Elle tenait peu à sa réputation et beaucoup à sa gloire. Sembler facile et être impossible, voilà le chef-d'œuvre. Josiane se sentait majesté et matière. C'était une beauté encombrante. Elle empiétait plus qu'elle ne charmait. Elle marchait sur les cœurs. Elle était terrestre. On l'eût aussi étonnée de lui montrer une âme dans sa poitrine que de lui faire voir des ailes sur son dos. Elle dissertait sur Locke. Elle avait de la politesse. On la soupçonnait de savoir l'arabe."

In one sentence the author tells that she made much of Lord David's mistresses, and in the next that she is without spot or blemish. We can but believe that the most enthusiastic admirer of French literature will be completely disgusted with this intolerable nonsense. Even if such inconsistencies really existed in the human character, what possible good can come from the portrayal of them with such apparent relish and abandon?

The author's conception of his hero, Gwynplaine, is grotesque in the extreme. Gwynplaine was the son of a nobleman. The king wished to deprive him of his inheritance, and ordered him to be sold when two years of age, and employed a physician of Flanders to mutilate his features by performing an operation called "bucca fissa usque ad aures," which stamps an eternal laugh upon the face.

The whimsical exaggeration of this character is almost unendurable, but, however, some of the scenes in which he is an actor are strikingly portrayed; for instance, the terrible scene in the House of Lords, where he is made to endure the scorn of his brother peers.

We give the following description of a storm at sea as a

specimen of the author's wild extravagance and quaint and ridiculous illustrations :

"Where the ocean was free from foam it had a sticky appearance. The waves, losing their sharp edges in the twilight, looked like puddles of gall. Here and there a flattened billow showed cracks and stars like a window at which stones had been thrown. At the centre of these stars, in eddying apertures, trembled a phosphorescence which recalled the cat-like after-gleam of departed life in a screech-owl's eyes."

The denouement of this novel is fully in keeping with the style in which it is written. Josiane is never heard of after the memorable interview with Gwynplaine, in which she threw herself with the bound of a panther upon his neck, and told him in words which came out "pell-mell, like an eruption," that "she idolised him because she disdained him," that "she loved him because he was grotesque, hideous," and "that he was exquisite because he was infamous."

Dea dies from excess of joy at the return of her lover, and Gwynplaine puts an end to his miserable existence by drowning himself.

The absurdity of this novel we think destroys the very interest it was intended to create. The author speaks of writing two other books of the same character, to be entitled "Monarchy" and "Ninety-three." We hope, however, that he will abandon the idea. His genius is fitted for something better.

Marmontel's Belisarius.

Marmontel's *Belisarius* was written in 1777. As a literary production, it ranks far below *Les Contes Moraux* and *Les Incas*. The author claims to have relied wholly upon the faith of history for the material of his work. He quotes extensively in the introductory chapter from the writings of Procopius, and cites, we think, some very excellent reasons for not attributing to that historian a work entitled "Anecdotes of Secret History." Gibbon, Lebeau, and Guizot regard the book as genuine, though it is said that it does not conform with the author's style and diction, and that it was not even attributed to him until 500 years after his death. Agathias, and other contemporary historians, enumerate his works without mentioning it. This work is full of the most disgusting accounts of court intrigues and scandals. It contains a number of stories about Belisarius' relations almost as ridiculous and improbable as Harriet Beecher Stowe's revelations of Lord Byron.

It is a matter of regret that so little is known in regard to the last days of Belisarius. Gibbon, in the *Decline and Fall of the Roman Empire*, devotes considerable space to the military achievements of this great warrior, but for some unaccountable reason passes hurriedly over many important events which took place towards the close of his life. Had Gibbon examined these events with his accustomed care and fidelity, much light doubtless would have been thrown upon this interesting period of Roman history. Lord Mahon attempted to repair the deficiency, but his genius and scholarship were inadequate to the task, although he devoted much energy and research to it. He examined minutely the writings of Crinitus, Volaterranus, Pontanus, Marcellinus, and Ignatius, to say nothing of those of Procopius, Thucydides, Agathias, and Livy. He also brought forward information from a work hitherto unpublished, the four books descriptive of the city of Constantinople inserted in Bandun's *Imperium Orientale*, for the purpose of settling the vexed question of BELISARIUS' blindness and mendicity. Milman, however, in his notes on Gibbon, refuses to credit the testimony, and says that all accounts of BELISARIUS' blunders are fabled and entitled to no earthly consideration.

BELISARIUS was born on the confines of Thrace and Illyria about 500 years after Christ. In early youth he was distinguished as a warrior, and when only 25 years of age he was named Governor of Dara. A few years later he was chosen general of the Roman forces in the East. In 531 he won the famous battle of Callinicum. In 533 he undertook an expedition into Africa. It was crowned with the most brilliant success. He besieged the heroic Gelimer on the mountain of Papua. The Vandal chief made a determined resistance. He was reduced to sufferings and hardships of indescribable horror. His army was compelled to subsist in the midst of winter on the coarsest oaten cakes baked in ashes. The half-starved soldiers were even ready to devour their women and children. In the midst of this terrible distress the Vandal monarch displayed the loftiest courage and fortitude. He had been accustomed to the most luxurious pleasures, and the récollection of them, as may readily be imagined, only served to heighten his sufferings. In a letter to Pharas (the besieging commander), imploring mercy, he exclaims, "I have been suddenly cast from the throne into the abyss of misery. Justinian is a man and an emperor: does he not fear for himself a similar reverse of fortune? Send me, I pray you, to solace my sorrows, a lyre, a sponge, and a loaf of bread." The request was granted, but the besieging army only redoubled its vigilance, and the unfortunate king was compelled to capitulate. He was led in triumph to Constantinople in company with his wife and children, and a long train of Vandal nobles. The capital had never witnessed before such a magnificent procession. As the triumphal car moved from the palace of BELISARIUS toward the gates of the Hippodrome, the enthusiasm of the populace exceeded all bounds. It seemed as if all the wealth of the African continent was displayed. Jewelled thrones, glittering armor, costly vases and statues, and the magnificent chariots which had been used by the Vandal kings, composed part of the conqueror's procession. Gelimer, with dejected countenance, advanced slowly on foot, clothed in a robe of purple and gold. He maintained the utmost dignity of demeanor. Not a tear glistened in his eye, nor a single sigh was heaved from his manly breast. He is said to have derived a melancholy pleasure in repeating the words of Solomon, "Vanity of vanities, all is vanity."

BELISARIUS nobly refused to ride in the triumphal car, but walked modestly by the side of his brave comrades. As the procession approached the throne on which were seated the Emperor and Empress, the victorious general and captive hero were compelled to prostrate themselves on the ground and kiss the royal footstool.

BELISARIUS was now made the First Consul of the Empire, but Justinian soon became jealous of him, and waited only for a pretext to accomplish his ruin. In 542 he sequestered his estates and degraded him from the rank of a General.

His crime seems to have been simply the expression of an opinion that the Emperor's nearest kinsman should succeed to the throne instead of Theodora.

As BELISARIUS entered the city of Constantinople with his small and squalid retinue, the ungrateful people received him with insults and scoffings. He was made a prisoner in his own palace, and expected every moment either to fall by the hands of an assassin or to receive from the Emperor a sentence of death. At this time the Empire was threatened with invasion, and BELISARIUS was reinstated in his command.

His victories were more brilliant than ever; but they excited the bitterest jealousy at the Imperial Court, and he was again recalled and disgraced. His last victory was won at Chettos, in 559, against the Bulgarians. In 563 he was accused of being engaged in a conspiracy with Marcellus Sergius and others to murder the Emperor. Justinian was weak enough to believe the accusation, and ordered him under arrest.

Here Gibbon and other historians leave us in doubt as to the real facts of BELISARIUS' fate. It is said that the Emperor on account of BELISARIUS' past services, spared his life; but in accordance with an existing custom at the Byzantine Court, decreed that his eyes should be put out, and deprived him of all means of support by confiscating his property. There is a tradition that he was reduced to beg his bread from door to door, and that he held forth a platter of wood or earthenware for charity, with the plea, "Give a penny to the old soldier — to poor and blind Belisarius."

One of the most singular things in Marmontel's romance, is the view he has taken of Justinian. He says that the Emperor was a wise and virtuous man, and raised himself by his valor from the lowest station in the army to the Imperial throne. He also represents him as having done everything in his power to atone for the ruin he inflicted upon BELISARIUS in decreeing his eyes to be put out.

This position is entirely inconsistent with the character of one who, according to Gibbon and other historians, was an upstart monarch, who scarcely ever unsheathed his sword, and who shared his crown with a public prostitute, the vilest of her sex.

Marmontel's romance contains some very fine passages, but upon the whole it is dull and tedious. He represents BELISARIUS as conversing most eloquently upon such subjects as moral and ethical philosophy, the science of government, and the art of war; but many of the specimens he gives are full of weak and wishywashy sentiments.

We have endeavored to translate, as literally as possible, what we regard as the finest chapter in the book.

BELISARIUS directed his steps toward an old castle in ruins, where his family expected him. He was compelled to beg alms as he went. His dignified bearing and lofty expression of countenance could not do otherwise than attract the attention of the beholders, but he warned his guide not to reveal his name upon the route. In passing through a village he stopped in the evening at the door of a neat but plain-looking house. The owner of the dwelling was just returning home with a spade in his hand. He was struck with the noble appearance of BELISARIUS, and asked him who he was. The latter replied, "I am a poor old soldier." "A soldier!" exclaimed the villager; "and is this your reward?" "It is the misfortune of a sovereign," said BELISARIUS, "not to be able to reward all those who have fought in his service."

This reply touched the heart of the villager, and he begged him to accept his hospitality. "I introduce to you," said the master of the house to his wife, "a brave soldier, who supports courageously the severest trials of affliction." He then addressed BELISARIUS, saying, " Be not ashamed of your condition, for we too have experienced misfortune. I pray you be seated while supper is being prepared, and tell me in what wars you have served." " In the wars of Italy," said BELISARIUS, " against the Goths, and in those of Asia, against the Persians, and in those of Africa, against the Vandals and the Moors." At these last words the villager was not able to suppress a deep sigh. He said, "You have, then, made all the campaigns with BELISARIUS, who exhibited ever the utmost purity of heart and grandeur of intellect. In my retirement I have not heard from him for a quarter of a century. I hope he is still living, and that Heaven will bless and prolong his days."

BELISARIUS answered, " He is still living ; but if he could hear you he would be deeply moved at your kind wishes." " Then," said the villager, " how is he at court? All powerful, adored by every one?" "Alas!" replied his guest, " do you not know that envy ever attaches itself to greatness?" "Very true ; but the Emperor should be upon his guard in listening to the enemies of so great a man. He was the tutelar genius and the protector of the Empire. He is very old, but no matter; he would still be as great in the council as he was in the field."

BELISARIUS was now convinced that his host was some officer whom he had rewarded while in the army. During supper the latter was inquisitive about the wars in Italy and in the East, but did not refer to those of Africa. "Let us drink," said the host, at the conclusion of the repast, " to the health of your General. May Heaven not be unkind to him for the evil he inflicted upon me." " How did he ever injure you?" said BELISARIUS. " He discharged his duty; I do not complain; I have learned how to bear up under adversity. Since you have served in the African wars, you have doubtless seen the King of the Vandals, the unfortunate Gelimer, with his captive wife and children, led in triumph by BELISARIUS to Constantinople, I must tell you that I am Gelimer, the unfortunate King of the Vandals." "Are you, then, indeed, Gelimer?" said BELISARIUS. "Is it possible that the Emperor has made your lot so humble?" "The Emperor offered me honors, and I refused them. When one has been a king, and ceases to be a king, he has no recompense save in repose and obscurity. Yes, I was besieged upon the mountain of Papua. There I suffered hardships unheard of. In the midst of the severest winter I felt the pangs of hunger, and beheld the awful spectacle of a nation driven to despair and ready to devour their women and children. The vigilance of the brave Pharas was unremitting, but he did everything to direct my attention to the miserable condition of my people. This, together with the confidence I had in the integrity of your General, led me to lay down my arms.

"BELISARIUS received me with the greatest dignity. Every attention was paid to me. He did everything he could to console me in my affliction. I have passed six lusters in retirement, but each and every day I have offered up a fervent prayer for BELISARIUS. Before the surrender I had lived the most voluptuous of kings. I was nursed as it were in the lap of pleasure. Suddenly I passed from my palace to the cavern of the Moors, slept upon straw, and lived upon barley coarsely pounded and half washed upon cinders. Nay, to such hardships was I reduced that a loaf of bread sent to me by the enemy was a present inestimable. I was loaded with chains, and compelled to walk in the conqueror's triumph. After undergoing such affliction the heart must either break with grief or rise superior to it."

BELISARIUS replied, "You have in the composure of your soul many resources against calamity, and I promise before we part to give you a further consolation."

Early the next morning Gelimer found his guest with stick in hand ready to set out upon his journey. He begged him to pass a few days longer with him. BELISARIUS replied, "I have a wife and daughter inconsolable during my absence. Farewell! but hear unmoved what I have to reveal — BELISARIUS, though old and blind, will never forget the reception you have given him."

"Merciful Heaven!" exclaimed Gelimer; "BELISARIUS blind, and in his old age abandoned?".

"Yes; my enemies, before they reduced me to poverty, put out my eyes."

"Oh, just Heaven! who were the monsters?"

"The *envious*," said BELISARIUS. "They accused me of aspiring to the throne, when I thought only of the grave. They had the power to ruin me. I was placed in irons, but the people clamored for my deliverance. It was impossible to resist them; but, in restoring me to liberty, I was deprived of my sight; and Justinian ordered it. It was that that most pained me. You know with what zeal, with what love, and with what fidelity I served him. Even now I feel no anger toward him, and I deeply regret that he is surrounded by wicked men to darken the evening of his days. When I heard that he had pronounced the fatal sentence, I must confess that my constancy failed me. My executioner melted into pity and fell prostrate at my feet. Thanks be to Heaven! it is over now, and I have but a little while to be blind and poor."

Gelimer now asked BELISARIUS to pass the remainder of his life with him.

Belisarius replied: "It would indeed be consoling, but I owe a duty to my wife and children, and I go to die in their arms."

Gelimer embraced him with tears. He at last parted from him with the utmost difficulty; but watched him with longing eyes, and exclaimed, "O prosperity! O prosperity! who can confide in thee?"

VATHEK.

THIS celebrated Oriental story was written at one sitting, in French, by Sir WILLIAM BECKFORD, of Fonthill, England, when about eighteen years of age.

It abounds in scenes of surpassing beauty and magnificence. Its splendor of description, varied liveliness of humor, gorgeous richness. of fancy, and wild and supernatural interest, are perhaps unequaled in the whole range of fictitious literature. It seems as if all the sweets of Asia are poured out upon it. It is full of glittering palaces, and temples and towers, of jewelled halls, tables of agate and cabinets of ebony and pearl; of crystal fountains, radiant columns, and arcades and perfumes burning in censers of gold.

Lord Byron says, that " even Rasselas must bow before it, and the Happy Valley will not bear a comparison with the Hall of Eblis."

It is pervaded by an awful spirit of mockery and derision, which contrasts strangely with the author's reflections at the conclusion of the story.

The history of the author's life is scarcely less wonderful than his book. He was the son of Sir William Beckford, a prominent English statesman in the time of George III. The elder Beckford distinguished himself by a speech addressed to the King, in which he dared to upbraid his counsellors, and to denounce them as enemies to the constitution and laws of the country. The city of London erected a statue to his memory, with the speech engraved upon the pedestal.

The fortune he left his son was of the largest in England. His income was more than half a million dollars per annum. Young BECKFORD early displayed talents of the highest order. His education was conducted by some of the most eminent men of the nation. The Earl of Chatham and Lord Camden directed his studies in literature and philosophy, and Mozart instructed him in the science of music. He was not only versed in the classics, but was enabled to speak and write in nearly all the living languages of the earth, including the Persian and the Arabic. He endeavored to make himself familiar with every branch of science. He studied not only the natural, but the supernatural, the possible and the fantastical. He wrote, when but seventeen years of age, "The Memoirs of Extraordinary Painters," a work in which the richest humor and the keenest powers of sarcasm are displayed. He is also author of a brilliant series of letters entitled, "Italy, with Sketches of Spain and Portugal," and a work called "Recollections of an Excursion to the Monasteries of Alcobaca and Batalha."

In 1794 he removed to Portugal and constructed a magnificent palace at Cintra, which was allowed to go to destruction on his return to England. It suggested the following reflections in *Childe Harold:*

> "There, thou too, Vathek! England's wealthiest son,
> Once formed thy paradise, as not aware,
> When wanton wealth her mightiest deeds hath done,
> Meek peace voluptuous lures was ever wont to shun;
> Here didst thou dwell, here schemes of pleasure plan,
> Beneath yon mountain's ever beauteous brow.

> But now, as if a thing unblest by man,
> Thy fairy dwelling is as lone as thou ;
> Here giant weeds a passage scarce allow,
> To halls deserted, portals gaping wide ;
> Fresh lessons to the thinking bosom, how
> Vain are the pleasurances on earth supplied,
> Swept into wrecks anon by Time's ungentle tide."

He seemed to live only to "realise the dreams and fictions of his fancy." He had as great a passion for building palaces and towers as VATHEK himself. It is said that he embodied in his residence at Fonthill much of the splendor of the Hall of Eblis. The magnificent mansion erected by his father at a cost of nearly a million dollars failed to satisfy his fastidious taste. He had it pulled down, and built upon its ruins a palace famed throughout the world for its architectural beauty and costly magnificence. This wondrous structure seemed to spring into existence as if by enchantment. He employed four hundred and sixty men to work upon it by day and night. It is said that at one time every cart and wagon in the district were pressed into service, and that even the royal works of St. George's Chapel, Windsor, were abandoned in order to supply carpenters and masons to work upon it. The top of the building was inclosed in immense sweeps of plate glass. The central tower was two hundred and sixty-seven feet in height. It was indeed a palace of pleasure. Its decorations seemed to surpass the wildest dreams of Oriental splendor. The building was pushed forward with such rapidity that the foundation became insecure, and during a gust of wind the main tower fell to the earth.

Mr. BECKFORD was gifted with the most extraordinary vision. He gazed upon the sun with the eye of an eagle. He observed from a distance of forty miles, while on au eminence at Bath, that his tower had disappeared, and made known the fact to his friends before the news of its destruction arrived from Fonthill.

He then erected another palatial tower, which, if possible, surpassed the former in beauty and magnificence. Its furniture beggared description. The spacious saloons were crowded with the rarest treasures of art. He had three hundred and sixty different sets of tableware, one for each day during the year, of the costliest material.

He lived in this fairy dwelling in the utmost seclusion. It was seldom that any one ever beheld the splendors of his home. On one occasion the Duchess of Norfolk visited him. She was entertained for a week with the most varied and splendid generosity, but the owner of the mansion kept himself savagely inaccessible.

At one time he had a hideous and an emasculated Oriental dwarf attached to his person, after the fashion of the Asiatic princes. This eccentricity, together with his boundless wealth and secluded life, occasioned the ignorant and superstitious to believe that he was leagued with the devil and possessed the secrets of alchemy.

Vathek was first published in 1786. It was followed shortly afterward by an English translation, now included in Bohn's Standard Library. It has never been republished in this country. A brief outline of the plot cannot fail to be of interest to the reader.

VATHEK was the ninth Caliph of the race of the Abassides. He surpassed in magnificence all his predecessors. His dominions extended from Africa to India. His personal appearance was the very embodiment of majesty and dignity, but, when angry, one of his eyes became so terrible that no one could behold it and live. He was addicted to every pleasure and every vice. He was skilled in the occult sciences. He consulted the stars and penetrated into the profoundest mysteries of the soul. His palace commanded the whole city of Samarah, but it was too meagre to satisfy his vanity, and he erected five other palaces, designed for the gratification of each of the senses. The first was called the Eternal or the Unsatiating Banquet. Here the most delicious wines and cordials flowed from a hundred inexhaustible fountains. The second palace was styled the Temple of Melody or the Nectar of the Soul. It was frequented by the most distinguished poets and musicians of the land, who caused even "the surrounding scenery to reverberate with song." The third palace was termed the Delight of the Eyes or the Support of Memory. In it was collected everything that could possibly tend to dazzle and bewilder the senses. "Here a well-managed perspective attracted the sight, there the magic of optics agreeably deceived it, whilst the naturalist on his part exhibited in their several classes the various gifts that Heaven had bestowed on our globe." The two remaining palaces were called the Palace of Perfumes and the Retreat of Mirth. The latter was ever graced with "troops of young females as beautiful as the Houris and not less seducing."

VATHEK's subjects, notwithstanding his excesses, wished for him a long and happy reign. His pride reached its height and wickedness ran riot in him. He sullied himself with a thousand crimes. The Prophet Mahomet beheld his conduct with indignation, and resolved to leave him to his fate, and to see where his folly and impiety would lead him.

VATHEK determined to construct a tower, not in imitation of Nimrod, but for the purpose of penetrating the secrets of heaven. He fancied that even insensible matter showed a forwardness to subserve his designs, for when a cubit was raised in a day two cubits would be added at night.

It is said that when he ascended for the first time the fifteen hundred stairs of his tower, and looked down upon men no larger than pismires, and mountains than shells, and cities than bee-hives, he would have adored himself had he not looked upward and saw that the stars were as far above him as they appeared when he stood on the surface of the earth. He soon became the prey of a malignant giaour who promised him the diadem of Gian Ben Gian, the talismans of Solomon, and the treasures of the pre-Adamite kings.

His mother, Carathis, the most perfect incarnation of crime, fired his ambition to this end. Under the guidance of the giaour, he started to seek the treasures. "He trod upon the cloth of gold spread for his feet, and ascended his litter amidst the general acclamations of his subjects." His expedition was interrupted by portentous omens, such as darkness, fire, and tempest, and became lost in the mountains. He was met by two dwarfs who conducted him to the delightful retreat of the good Emir Fakreddin, in the midst of a valley of fruits, melons and flowers. Here he met the young and lovely Nouronihar, and persuaded her to accompany him to the palace of fire, and to share with him the honor and glory of his crown.

At last they beheld the darkened summits of Istakar. A benificent spirit in the form of a shepherd appeared, and warned them that beyond the mountains, Eblis and his accursed Dives held their infernal fire. The spirit informed VATHEK that but one moment of grace was allowed him, that when the sun passed from behind a cloud, if his heart was not changed he would be lost forever.

The Caliph scorned the advice and exclaimed, "Let the sun appear. Let him illumine my career. It matters not where it may end." Nouronihar importuned him to hasten his march, and lavished on him a thousand caresses to beguile reflection.

The ruins of Istakar were revealed to them, and they proudly entered its gloomy watch-towers.

After passing through a labyrinth of horrors interspersed with flitting visions of delight, they beheld an immense hall in which "a vast multitude was incessantly passing, who severally kept their right hands on their hearts, without once regarding any one around them. They had all the livid paleness of death. Their eyes deep sunk in their sockets, resembled those phosphoric meteors that glimmer by night in places of interment. Some stalked slowly on, absorbed in profound reverie, some shrieking with agony ran furiously about like tigers wounded with poisoned arrows, whilst others grinding their teeth in rage, foamed along more frantic than the wildest maniac. They all avoided each other, and though surrounded by a multitude which no one could number, each wandered at random unheedful of the rest, as if alone on a desert where no foot had trodden."

VATHEK and Nouronihar, though frozen with terror at this sight, moved on until they reached the throne of Soliman. As the mighty potentate raised his hand to heaven in token of supplication, they discerned through his bosom, which was transparent as crystal, his heart enveloped in flames.

VATHEK and his companions were informed that a like fate awaited them, and "their hearts immediately took fire, and they at once lost the most precious gift of Heaven — Hope."

This scene belongs to the highest order of intellectual poetry. There is nothing in Dante or Milton that surpasses it in grandeur, power and sublimity.

Mr. BECKFORD lived to the advanced age of 84. His intellect remained unclouded to the last. His fame as an author, however, rests principally upon his earlier productions. His letters in which he gives an account of his travels, were not published until fifty years after they were written. He employed the last years of his life in collecting treasures for his residence at Bath, where he united two houses in London Crescent by an arch thrown from one street to another, in which he placed his library, which was one of the best selected and most extensive in England.

The Tempest.

SHAKSPEARE was indebted solely to the inspiration of his genius for the material of this exquisite creation. His critics and commentators have wholly failed to trace the origin of the plot to any other source. The poet Collins, however, claimed that it was founded upon a romance entitled "Amelia and Isabella," printed in the Italian, Spanish, French, and English, in 1588. There is nothing, however, in "Amelia and Isabella," not even the faintest outline, to warrant such a conclusion. Warton, in commenting upon the above, says that Collins had searched the subject with no less fidelity than judgment and industry; but during a moment of mental aberration probably gave the name of one novel for another. Warton also expresses the opinion that the original novel will yet be discovered, inasmuch as Collins mentions that the principal character of the romance answering to Shakspeare's Prospero was a chemical necromancer, who had bound a spirit like Ariel to obey his call and perform his services.

Tieck earnestly maintains that the TEMPEST was taken from an Italian drama, of which a German version is preserved in Ayer's play entitled *Die Schöne Sidea* (the Beauful Sidea). His arguments are based principally upon some striking points of resemblance between the two plays; but as the earlier drama is not known to exist, it is probable that the Beautiful Sidea is only an adaptation or imitation of the TEMPEST.

SHAKSPEARE'S reference to "the still vex'd Bermoothes" has given rise to the opinion that the scene of the drama was laid in the Bermudas.

Sir George Somers, who was wrecked upon one of these isles, published an account of his voyage about three years before the play was written, in which he gave a glowing description of this land of enchantment, of groves of coral, of perpetual blossoms and ever verdant bowers. The poet doubtless had read the account of this voyage, and had had the Bermudas in his mind's eye; but Ariel's flight from "a nook of the isle" to "fetch dew" from "the still vex'd Bermoothes," is, we think, a convincing proof that the isles were some distance from the scene of the drama.

The TEMPEST has often been compared with the "Midsummer-Night's Dream." The contrast between the real and the ideal, the natural and the supernatural, in both of these dramas, is unquestionably carried to a greater extent than in any other of the author's productions. The two plays, however, are too widely dissimilar to admit of any general comparison. The "Midsummer-Night's Dream" is perhaps adorned with the fairest flowers of poetry, and the most exquisite and delicate word-paintings, and the most varied and complicated confusions of beauties; but the TEMPEST possesses a greater unity of effect, and a greater combination of thought and interest, and a more harmonious blending of opposite elements.

It also possesses more depth of feeling, affection and sentiment, and a more refined and contemplative philosophy. The TEMPEST is generally regarded as the finest play, and the "Midsummer-Night's Dream" as the finest poem.

In the character of Ariel we have a beautiful exhibition of the poet's power for giving form and distinctness to winged and immortal beings. Ariel is called "the featureless angel." He hurries to and fro with the swiftness of thought, and drinks the air before him. We have scarcely time to look at him in one shape before we see him in another. He is as frolicsome and mischievous as he is bright and ethereal. He does all his spiriting gently, and is too delicate to act earthly, and abhors commands. It matters not how he presents himself to our fancy, either as a water-nymph or a harpy, or "sleeping in a cowslip's bell," or "imprisoned in a cloven pine," or "diving into the fire" or "into the salt sea," or "riding upon the curled clouds," or "living in the colors of the rainbow," or "running upon the sharp wind of the north," or "flying upon the bat's back, after summer merrily," or "refusing to do his master's strong bidding," he seems ever the same self-consistent being, kindling thoughts to wander throughout eternity.

We confess our inability to analyse the character of Caliban. He is something *infrahuman*, a mixture of man, brute, and devil, and yet in no way presents the distinctive elements of either. Monster as he is, he is sensible to kindness, and endeavors to show his gratitude as best his savage nature will allow him. He says to Prospero:

> "When thou cam'st here first
> Thou strok'dst me and made much of me; wouldst give me
> Water with berries in't, and teach me how
> To name the bigger light, and how the less
> That burn by day and night, and then I lov'd thee,
> And show'd thee all the qualities o' the isle,
> The fresh springs, brine pits, barren places and fertile."

His mind has been compared to a dark cave through which the rays of light serve not to warm or illumine, but to set in motion the poisonous vapors that generate in it.

His malignity is easily aroused, and when it is he cares only for the use of language to vent the deepest curses.

Prospero moves through the diverse elements of the

Tempest with unequaled power and beauty and wisdom. His high charms work only for the noblest and most praiseworthy ends.

Shakspeare has chosen him to utter two of the finest passages of poetry in the drama. It is almost unnecessary to say that we mean the description of the disappearance of the vision he has conjured up, and the speech where he abjures his art and proposes to break his staff and bury it "fathoms in the earth," and drown his book

"Deeper than did ever plummet sound."

The former is so full of poetic splendor that we cannot resist reproducing it here :

> "Our revels now are ended. These, our actors,
> As I foretold you, were all spirits, and
> Are melted into air, into thin air;
> And, like the baseless fabric of this vision,
> The cloud-capp'd towers, the gorgeous palaces,
> The solemn temples, the great globe itself,
> Yea, all which it inherit, shall dissolve,
> And, like this unsubstantial pageant, faded,
> Leave not a rack behind. We are such stuff
> As dreams are made on, and our little life
> Is rounded with a sleep."

Miranda is the most purely ideal of all Shakspeare's women. She seems to belong to a higher order of beings than of this earth. All the aerial splendor and magical mystery of her father's isle seem to be interwoven in her nature, and yet she is as distinct and palpable a creation as if she actually existed in real life. She has no acquired or artificial manners, and is totally ignorant of the false notions of society that teach us to flatter and dissemble. Modesty, and truth, and honor, and purity, and virtue, and nnocence, are her dower. She never saw one of her own sex, and has grown up with no companions save her father, and the ministering spirits of the air and the rocks and trees and caves and dells and brooks and fountains of her fairy home. Her heart swells with filial affection and all the attending virtues of holy innocence. She is a celestial being, breathing thoughtful breath. She sees everything through her own hallowed imagination. Even Caliban is to her simply "a villain she does not love to look on." No wonder Ferdinand approaches her as something above the earth earthy, as "a goddess upon whom the airs attend."

The courtship between her and Ferdinand is managed with exquisite grace and delicacy.

> "At the first sight
> They have changed eyes."

We cannot imagine anything more beautiful than the following extracts from the third act:

> FER.—"Full many a lady
> I have ey'd with best regard; and many a time
> The harmony of their tongues hath into bondage
> Brought my too diligent ear. For several virtues
> Have I lik'd several women; never any
> With so full soul, but some defect in her
> Did quarrel with the noblest grace she ow'd
> And put it to the foil: But you, O, you
> So perfect and so peerless, are created
> Of every creature's best."

* * * * * * * *

> "Wherefore weep you?"
> MIRA.—"At mine own unworthiness, that dare not offer
> What I desire to give, and much less take
> What I shall die to want: But this is trifling;
> And all the more it seeks to hide itself,
> The bigger bulk it shows. Hence, bashful cunning,
> And prompt me plain and holy innocence!
> I am your wife, if you will marry me;
> If not, I'll die your maid. To be your fellow,
> You may deny me; but I'll be your servant,
> Whether you will or no."

The Scarlet Letter.

Hawthorne is, we think, the ablest writer of pure fiction in the language. There is nothing commonplace about him. Unlike most novelists, he deals less with accidental manifestations than with universal principles. His characters are not mere shadowy abstractions, but "veritable human souls, though dwelling in a far-off world of cloud-land." He is a purist in style, and is at all times as scrupulously exact in his choice of words as if he were writing a complete and perfect poem. All his works, from his earliest productions, the "Twice Told Tales," to his later efforts, the "Marble Faun" and "Our Old Home," bear upon them the ineffaceable stamp of genius, and ever awaken ideas of beauty, of solemnity, and of grandeur. The Scarlet Letter is perhaps his greatest creation.

There is a suggestiveness and an originality about it for which we may search in vain for a parallel outside of the writings of Shakspeare. In it he penetrates into the recesses of the heart, and touches the secret springs of our inmost passions and desires. It is a deep, a strange, a profound and an awful tragedy, in which the severest and most appalling sufferings known to man are not only depicted with wonderful naturalness and intensity, but laid bare as it were to the gaze even of persons of the dullest and most unimaginative sensibilities. Hawthorne is said to have derived his first conception of this story from reading a sentence written upon an old yellow parchment, accidentally found among some rubbish in the Custom-house at Boston, decreeing that a woman convicted of adultery should stand upon the platform of a pillory in front of the market-place with the letter "A" written on her breast. A friend who saw him read it remarked to a gentleman standing near: "We shall hear, I am sure, of the letter 'A' again." HAWTHORNE, in the introductory chapter to the romance, not only relates the story of reading the sentence, but says that he actually found a piece of fine red cloth, much worn and faded by time and wear, in the shape of the letter "A," and that he involuntarily put it upon his breast, and seemed to experience a sensation of burning heat, as if the letter were not of scarlet cloth but of red-hot iron, and that he shuddered and let it fall upon the floor. He added that it was the subject of meditation for many an hour while pacing to and fro across his room, or traversing with a hundred-fold repetition the long extent from the front door of the Custom-house to the side entrance and back again. He felt there was a mystic and a terrible meaning in it most worthy of interpretation.

The interpretation he gave will endure forever. He has portrayed, as no one else could portray, the religious faith of the Puritans. In depicting it in all its hideous deformity, he does not exaggerate anything or conceal anything. Its victim, Hester Prynne, whether whether or not a true type of her class, must forever be associated with the intolerance, narrow prejudices and vindictive feelings of the bigoted sect who thought themselves especially chosen by Heaven to punish the guilty with the most damnable instruments of torture. The author, in discoursing upon the hard and unyielding severity of their laws, never allows his indignation to overmaster his judgment. In the very whirlwind of passion he begets a temperance which gives it smoothness. It has been urged as an objectionable feature in his writings that he does not solve moral and psychological problems, "but exhibits their bearings and workings in concrete and living forms, for experiment and illustration." Now this is exactly what we most admire in him. It is a part of the peculiarity of genius not to be decisive, to raise questions rather than to settle them. HAWTHORNE seems to care more for giving his readers an opportunity of discovering truth themselves than to point it out to them. But sometimes, we admit, he abuses this power; for instance, when he refuses to tell us in the "Marble Faun" whether Donatello has pointed and furry ears or not, or where he excites our curiosity by concealing the cause of the influence of the ill-omened Capuchin over the courageous and noble-hearted Miriam; or in the following comparison of hatred and love in the SCARLET LETTER: "It is a curious subject of observation and inquiry whether hatred or love be not the same thing at bottom. Each in its utmost development supposes a high degree of intimacy and heart-knowledge; each renders one individual dependent for the food of his affections and spiritual life upon another; each leaves the passionate lover, or the no less passionate hater, forlorn and desolate by the withdrawal of his subject. Philosophically considered, therefore, the two passions seem essentially the same, except that one happens to be seen in a celestial radiance, and the other in a dusky and lurid glow."

There is something about HAWTHORNE'S children that affects us with singular love and admiration. They are not prodigies, like Paul Dombey and Elinor Trench, but have all the natural bloom, freshness and simplicity of childhood. They are imbued with a spell of infinite variety. They breathe an atmosphere of love and beauty, of enchanting hopes and dreams. We feel that theirs is the only flowery path, the golden period of existence, the unclouded dawn of life. We do not find anything inconsistent even in the conduct of little Pearl, one of the most shadowy, ethereal and mystical of all his creations, when we recollect that "she seemed the unpremeditated offshoot of a passionate moment," and that "the child's nature had something wrong in it, which continually betokened that she had been born amiss, the effluence of her mother's lawless passion;" indeed, we except the terrible scene at the brook side, where she refused to come to her mother, though called in accents of honeyed sweetness, until she placed the scarlet letter upon her breast, but stood motionless, pointing with her finger where she was accustomed to see it. The author, however, endeavors to reconcile her conduct in the following: "Children will not abide any, the slightest change in the accustomed aspect of things that are daily before their eyes. Pearl misses something which she has always seen me wear."

We know of nothing in the whole range of literature that equals the sufferings of the mother when she again fastens the letter on her breast, feeling that she must bear the torture a while longer. "Hopefully but a moment ago as Hester had spoken of drowning it in the deep sea, there was a sense of inevitable doom upon her as she thus received back this deadly symbol from the hand of fate. She had flung it into infinite space! She had drawn an hour's free breath! and here again was the scarlet misery glittering on the old spot! So it ever is, whether thus typified or not, that an evil deed invests itself with the character of doom."

We have a hint at the conclusion of this mystical romance that little Pearl grew to womanhood, and that her wild, rich nature had been softened and subdued, and made capable of the gentlest happiness. The description of Hester's repentance is so full of divine philosophy that no one can rise from its perusal without a purer and deeper sympathy for the failings of humanity.

"But there was more real life for Hester Prynne, here in New England, than in that unknown region where Pearl had found a home. Here had been her sin; here, her sorrow; and here was yet to be her penitence. She had returned, therefore, and resumed, of her own free will, for not the sternest magistrate of that iron period would have imposed it — resumed the symbol of which we have related so dark a tale. Never afterwards did it quit her bosom. But, in the lapse of the toilsome, thoughtful, and self-devoted years that made up Hester's life, the scarlet letter ceased to be a stigma which attracted the world's scorn and bitterness, and became a type of something to be sorrowed over, and looked upon with awe, yet with reverence too. And as Hester Prynne had no selfish ends, nor lived in any measure for her own profit and enjoyment, people brought all their sorrows and perplexities, and besought her counsel, as one who had herself gone through a mighty trouble. Woman, more especially,— in the continually recurring trials of wounded, wasted, wronged, misplaced, or erring and sinful passion,— or with the dreary burden of a heart unyielded, because unvalued and unsought,— came to Hester's cottage, demanding why they were so wretched, and what the remedy! Hester comforted and counseled them, as best she might. She assured them, too, of her firm belief, that, at some brighter period, when the world should have grown ripe for it, in Heaven's own time, a new truth would be revealed, in order to establish the whole relation between man and woman on a surer ground of mutual happiness. Earlier in life,

Hester had vainly imagined that she herself might be the destined prophetess, but had long since recognised the impossibility that any mission of divine and mysterious truth should be confided to a woman stained with sin, bowed down with shame, or even burdened with a life-long sorrow. The angel and apostle of the coming revelation must be a woman, indeed, but lofty, pure, and beautiful; and wise, moreover, not through dusky grief, but the ethereal medium of joy; and showing how sacred love should make us happy, by the truest test of a life successful to such an end."

We regret that we cannot now give further extracts from this romance, illustrative of the author's delicate sentiment and mystical imagination, as well as of his suggestiveness and originality. He has the purest and loftiest ideas of love and virtue. Unlike Thackeray, he never indulges in petty and contemptible sneers at women, nor dwells with exquisite delight upon their timorous debasement and self-humiliation. He does not stop to prove that "they are born timid and tyrants," and are terrified into humility, and bullied and frightened into devotion.

Edwin Booth's Macbeth.

It has been said that many gifts and accomplishments must meet in him who would be a commentator upon Shakspeare; that in this case, to know something of everything, but everything of something, is necessary for success.

But great as are the attributes required of a commentator, incomparably greater must be the gifts of the actor of Shakspeare. He must be a being who can rise superior to time and place, for the thoughts and passions he is to express and delineate belong not only to the past and the present, but to the future. His mind must be capable of comprehending the arts and sciences. He must be versed not only in history, but in the philosophy of history. He must be a student of nature and a judge of nature, and, above all, of character. He must possess the quality of identifying himself with the being he is to personate. He must be his own teacher, for if he stoops to imitation he degrades his art. Hence it is that our greatest actors have been the greatest innovators on the customs and manners of others. The innovations of Garrick on the style of acting adopted by Quin and Betterton, were such as for a time to make him very unpopular. Kemble attempted to set up a school of his own, and in some respects succeeded. Both Garrick and Kemble were men of fine scholastic attainments, but the former, in spite of his many excellences, represented MACBETH as a blustering and cowardly tyrant, who thought only of blood and murder, as a being wholly destitute of any redeeming traits whatever.

Byron was accustomed to say that of actors Cooke was the most natural, Kemble the most supernatural, and Kean the medium between the two, and that Mrs. Siddons was worth them all put together. He did not, however, record any opinion of Junius Brutus Booth, who combined excellences that did not belong to any of the above-named. But, to judge from contemporaneous criticism, and the traditions of the stage, EDWIN BOOTH, the son of Junius Brutus, has surpassed in the power and brilliancy of his genius all the great actors who have gone before him. He seems to have taken the lovers of the drama, as it were, by storm. He has brought to bear upon his profession the rarest personal gifts and the most superior mental accomplishments. He has revealed beauties in Shakspeare that were undreamed of before. He has thrust aside old stage tricks and customs. He has shown us the folly of set speeches and pompous intonations. He has completely charmed us with the varied witchery of his powers. He has aspired to the universal in the realms of art and knowledge, and success has crowned his efforts. We can account very readily for his success in some of his characters, for instance, in Hamlet, for the character is not wholly unlike his own. His handsome person, elegant graces and quiet dignity, combined with his wealth of voice, are eminently fitted for the sublimest representations of this great conception of Shakspeare.

The mournful words,

"I have of late, but wherefore I know not,
Lost all my mirth, foregone all customs of exercises,"

seem to bespeak his own sentiments and passions. The

same thing can be said of the soliloquy on suicide, whilst the friendship of Rosencranz and Guildenstern, the deferred but deeply-seated revenge, the wild love for Ophelia and the philosophical meditations at her grave, the chivalric bearing towards Laertes, the speech,

"If it be now, 'tis not to come; if it be not to come, it will be now; if it be not come yet, it will come. The readiness is all, since no man of aught knows what is't to leave betimes. Let be,"—

And all Hamlet's thoughts, speeches, words and actions are anything else but foreign to the proud and sensitive and philosophical and poetical nature of EDWIN BOOTH.

But by what wondrous power doth he transform himself into the bloody Thane of Cawdor, and fearlessly visit the blasted heath, invoke the magic spell of the weird sisters, look on death itself, and sleep in spite of thunder? The question must remain unanswered. It is inexplicable. We only know that it is the exclusive gift and prerogative of genius.

BOOTH studied the character of MACBETH thoroughly and completely before he attempted to portray it. His Hamlet, we believe, has been slowly perfected by study, time and thought; but there has been no improvement in his MACBETH since his appearance in the character, nor can there be any, for he mastered it from the beginning. If he does not play it as well at one time as at another, it is from sheer lack of physical force. He seizes at once upon the imagination, and holds us spell-bound until the end of the drama, and we cannot break the spell if we would.

His appearance upon the stage, heralded by distant strains of martial music, and the exclamation of the weird sisters,

"A drum! a drum! MACBETH doth come!"

presents a picture of the grandest magnificence. We

realise the approach of all the splendid pageantry of war and the glory of a conqueror. He is proudly followed by his victorious army, that beat back " Norway himself with terrible numbers." He surveys majestically their burnished shields, waving banners and glittering spears. His brow is flushed with triumph, and every look and movement bespeaks the conqueror, whose brandished sword but an hour before smoked with bloody execution:

The warlike cry —

"Command! they halt upon the heath!"

is distinctly heard. The pictured representation of that dreary moorland consecrated to infernal orgies, with not a tree or shrub to relieve the desolation, where murky fogs are ever settling upon pestilential pools, becomes a reality. How strangely sound the foreboding words,

" So fair and foul a day I have not seen!"

How prophetic of the coming evil, of the workings of the powers of darkness, of the weird sisters, the wild and secret midnight hags, who keep the word of promise to the ear and break it to the hope! Only those who have seen BOOTH'S MACBETH can form the least idea of the expression of his countenance on beholding the weird sisters. There is something about it that affects us with mingled admiration and awe. When these foul anomalies greet him as "Thane of Glamis," "Thane of Cawdor," and as " All hail Macbeth, that shall be King hereafter," we feel that he is indeed under the influence of superhuman beings, who are to control his destiny and urge him on to his fate. He seems to believe all their predictions possible. He does not listen, like Banquo, passively, neither begging nor fearing, but his whole being is moved. He is lost in thought; wrapped withal. When they are about to quit his sight, we hear with strange emotion the speech:

> "Stay, you imperfect speakers, tell me more.
> By Sinel's death, I know I am Thane of Glamis;
> But how of Cawdor? The Thane of Cawdor lives,
> A prosperous gentleman; and to be King
> Stands not within the prospect of belief,
> No more than to be Cawdor. Say from whence
> You owe this strange intelligence? or why
> Upon this blasted heath you stop our way
> With such prophetic greetings? Speak, I charge you."

But in order to appreciate fully his acting, we must follow MACBETH to the palace at Forres, where the things that did sound so fair have been partially realised, where the King of Scotland named him Thane of Cawdor, and

> "Two truths are told,
> As happy prologues to the swelling act
> Of the Imperial theme,"

and behold him break the intelligence to his wife of Duncan's promise to visit him at the castle of Inverness, that pleasant seat where heaven's breath smells wooingly, and where no jutty frieze, buttress, or coigne of vantage can heighten the mansion's beauty, for the temple-haunting martlets have there made their pendant beds and procreant cradles, but where the direst cruelty makes thick the blood, and stops up the access and passage to remorse.

BOOTH, in this scene with LADY MACBETH, makes us deeply sensible of all the hidden virtues of the character. The murder is resolved upon, but we read in his countenance waywardness and hesitancy. We know intuitively that he does not consent willingly to the unnatural deed, that he is full of the milk of human kindness, of the noblest sentiments and feelings, that he wishes to be great, but holily, and that which he fears to do he would wish undone. Although his thoughts are upon the golden round, he cannot look like the innocent flower and be the serpent under it. He has won golden opinions from all sorts of people, and he feels that they should be worn in their newest gloss. The King hath honored him of late, and now visits him in a double trust.

As a host and subject he feels that he should shut the door against the murderer, and not bear the knife himself.

We cannot describe the varied expressions of BOOTH's countenance when attempting to beat back the wicked impulses of LADY MACBETH, or his lofty bearing towards her when overcome by her reasoning, he says:

> "Bring forth men-children only,
> For thy undaunted metal should compose
> Nothing but males."

To have witnessed him in the scene previous to the murder of Duncan, forms, we think, an epoch in one's existence. In it he seems to surpass himself. If he is great in any other part of the play, he is almost superhuman in this. A darkness more terrible than nature's pervades the chamber through which he moves to kill the King. He does his utmost to dispel the supernatural vision, but cannot. The silence is dreadful. It is too painful to be borne. Each moment seems an eternity. We can almost hear his heart-throbs.

When the shadows proceeding from the heat-oppressed brain are dispelled, he indeed moves like a ghost, with "Tarquin's ravishing strides towards his design." But when the murder is committed, and he shows his bloodstained hands to his guilty wife, and exclaims,

> "This is a sorry sight!"

we are so lost in the character that we do not think once of the mighty genius that is portraying the mightiest effort of Shakspeare.

When he recites the following:

> "Methought I heard a voice cry, 'Sleep no more;
> Macbeth doth murder sleep;' the innocent sleep;
> Sleep, that knits up the ravel'd sleeve of care,
> The death of each day's life, sore labor's bath,
> Balm of hurt minds, great nature's second course,
> Chief nourisher in life's feast;
> Still it cried sleep no more to all the house;
> Glamis hath murdered sleep; and therefore Cawdor
> Shall sleep no more; MACBETH shall sleep no more"—

we feel indeed that the author's genius has here taken its full swing, and "trod upon the farthest bounds of nature and passion." But we do not feel all the terrible desperation of him who has given his eternal jewel to the common enemy of man, until the actor calls fate into the list to champion him to the very utterance.

What an infinite variety of contrasts he reveals to us in the banquet scene! Would that we could describe his imperial look, his smooth dissimulation in welcoming the guests, his conciousness of murder, and his unearthly horror on seeing the table full and his own chair occupied by him whose presence he had just affected to desire.

But when he cries out, with that wonderful and passionate intonation peculiarly his own,

> "Thou canst not say I did it! never shake
> Thy gory locks at me!
> Avaunt! quit my sight! Let the world hide thee!
> Thy bones are marrowless; thy blood is cold;
> Thou hast no speculation in the eyes
> Which thou dost glare with,"

we behold the sublimest description of impassioned terror.

It is well that the action of this play is so violent and the scenes so wonderfully varied, or else we should go mad with horror. The incidents are crowded together in rapid succession, and each rivals the other in magnitude and power. We are hurled hither and thither without guide or compass, through guilt and crime, darkness and despair. We are swayed to and fro as if by the power of fate. The central figure in this dense mass of chaotic confusion is MACBETH; around him every other interest must bend and break. He resolved to seek again the weird sisters, and to know the worse by the worst means; and with him we, too, long for their presence, for even the thoughts of their vile incantations, the grotesque strangeness of their charms — the grave from a murderer's gibbet, the finger of a baby strangled in its birth, the fillet of a fenny snake, the eye of newt and the toe of frog, the gall of a goat and the liver of a Jew, the blood of a baboon and the sweltering venom of other hideous ingredients — afford us a brief respite from the sufferings of such a conscience as BOOTH lays open to us.

In that part of the play where MACBETH grows more and more desperate, battling with fate, and even the season of all nature's calm can bring no rest to his weary soul, it is indeed melancholy in the extreme to behold the breathing impersonation of this gallant soldier, this wise leader, whose ambition was once guided and restrained by an instructed conscience, subjected to such vehement and tumultuous passions, and cut off from all hope and consolation, save such as he may derive from the double-meaning promises of the juggling fiends who are urging him on to destruction. The suffering of Vathek in the Hall of Eblis, under the cabalistic influence of the malignant giaour, forms scarcely a parallel. When there is nothing left for MACBETH save to abandon himself wholly to the power of the weird sisters, even though on horror's head horrors accumulate, we behold in the impersonation the loftiest energy and courage. He proudly descends the rugged steps that lead to the gloomy recesses of the cave, where the midnight hags are practising their incantations around a filthily seething cauldron. When he summons the spirits that know all mortal consequence to answer him "if Banquo's issue shall ever reign in the kingdom," BOOTH's acting reaches a degree of sublimity which can only be described as something above nature. When the shadows of eight kings pass before him, all like the spirit of Banquo, the prolonged and ringing intonations of his voice will be remembered for a lifetime, when he says:

> "What! will the line stretch out to the crack of doom?
> Another yet! A seventh! I'll see no more!
> And yet the eighth appears, who bears a glass
> Which shows me many more, and some I see
> That two-fold balls and treble sceptres carry.
> Horrible sight!— Now I see 'tis true,
> For the blood-boltered Banquo smiles upon me,
> And points at them for his!"

It is useless to multiply instances of his eloquent and masterly renditions of the text. What we most admire in him is that he makes the meaning of the author perfectly clear to us. What a singular anomaly of consistent inconsistencies he reveals in the character. He is sensible to pity, and is cruel and treacherous; he is kind and generous, and murders innocence and virtue. His imagination is lofty, and his energy is equal to his imagination, and his heroism is greater than both. His hatred is severe beyond measure, and his envy is intolerable; but his love of glory is unsurpassed, and ever throws a resplendent light around his vices and his crimes. All his purposes are broken and disjointed. Hope alternates with despair, and there is ever an appalling and a desperate struggle for the mastery.

One of the finest scenes in the play is where the death of his wife is announced.

The recollection of her delicate and unremitting attention to his conscience-stricken soul, the complacency with which she listened to his tempestuous wailings, without so much as the faintest murmur of her own sufferings, crowd upon him, and sicken his soul to the last faint echoes of moral death. He mourns her loss in all the terrible bitterness of his soul. BOOTH's recitation of the following beggars description:

> "She should have died hereafter;
> There would have been a time for such a word.
> To-morrow, and to-morrow, and to-morrow,
> Creeps in this petty pace from day to day,
> To the last syllable of recorded time;
> And all our yesterdays have lighted fools
> The way to dusty death. Out, out, brief candle,
> Life's but a waking shadow; a poor player,
> That struts and frets his hour upon the stage,
> And then is heard no more; it is a tale
> Told by an idiot, full of sound and fury,
> Signifying nothing—"

We know full well that LADY MACBETH is not "a mere female fury," though we both hate and fear her. She has been compared to Medea and to Clytemnestra, but she is infinitely more terrible than either of them, because she has more intellect, more passion and more refinement. She is free from selfishness, and has no petty vices, no low and vulgar passions, no indelicacy or gross licentiousness of character. She sacrificed every womanly feeling for the aggrandisement of her husband. If she longed for the crown and sceptre, it was only that she might share them with him "to give all their days and nights sole sovereign sway and masterdom." Great as was her crime, we feel that others have been more debasing, for, judge her as we may, there is something about her that must forever be associated with her sex and with humanity.

But we must hurry on to a conclusion. The combat scene is indescribable.

We behold indeed an awful grandeur in the conclusive throes and dying agonies of "valor's minion," of him who threw before his body his warlike shield, and would try the last, though "Birnam wood be come to Dunsinane," and being opposed by "none of woman born."

But we would suppress the shouts of the victorious Scots over the fallen hero, for fate and metaphysical aid conspired against him.

Percy Bysshe Shelley.

It is almost impossible to think of Shelley without feelings of the deepest sorrow. The many sad incidents in his brief life, his wild and restless disposition, his insane ideas of the Christian religion, and his sudden and horrible death, crowd upon us in mournful and rapid succession.

He was born on the 4th of August, 1792, at his father's residence, known as Field Place, in Sussex county, England.

Through an imperfect knowledge of the facts of his birth, he has been represented as a descendant of Sir Philip Sidney. His grandfather, Sir Bysshe Shelley, married (the last time) Miss Sidney Perry, who was a descendant of Sir Philip Sidney; but the poet's father, Timothy Shelley, sprang from a previous marriage. It is useless, however, to attempt to correct the error, for, like the mythical story of William Tell and the apple, it has passed into history. And, indeed, it seems almost a pity to spoil the fiction, for Shelley resembled Sidney — that "chivalric warbler in poetic prose"— somewhat in personal appearance, in dignity and elegance of demeanor, in refinement and cultivation of taste, and in magnanimity and nobleness of soul.

At the age of thirteen, Shelley was sent to Eton to prepare for a course of study at the University of Oxford. At Eton he made much progress in Latin and Greek, but at Oxford he neglected the regular course of study in order to gratify his taste in the science of metaphysics.

SHELLEY at this time had begun to compose in both prose and verse, and with some assistance, wrote several romances; but it was his misfortune to offend the dignity of the faculty of Oxford by writing a pamphlet in which he endeavored to prove the non-existence of a Deity. For this offence he was very foolishly expelled. The vain and weak judges attempted to justify his expulsion on the ground that it was in conformity with a statute which expressly provided that the presence of an atheist should not be tolerated within the walls of the University. This statute has, however, to the credit of this celebrated institution of learning, been repealed. It must have required the height of stupidity to suppose that the sublime teachings of the Christian religion, glittering, as it were, with all that is great and good since the world began, could be endangered by the erratic speculations of a youth scarcely eighteen years of age.

SHELLEY'S expulsion from college was a sad disappointment to his family. They believed that they were in some measure involved in his disgrace. His father refused to allow him to return home except on condition of his renunciation of his religious opinions. This he indignantly refused to do. He went to London, thoroughly convinced that he was a martyr to the most oppressive tyranny.

While in London, he formed the acquaintance of Harriet Westbrook, a lady young and beautiful, but who was beneath him in rank and social position, being the daughter of a tavern-keeper. Notwithstanding the most vehement opposition, he married her.

In 1812 SHELLEY went to Ireland. He immediately became interested in the cause of Irish freedom. He issued an address to the people, in which he deprecated the prevalence of the Catholic religion. He said that "the Inquisition was set up, and in the course of one year thirty thousand people were burnt in Spain for entertaining a different opinion from the Pope and the priests. The bigoted monks of France massacred, in one night, eighty thousand Protestants." He warned the people of Ireland to take care that while one tyranny was destroyed, another be not allowed to spring up. He told them to think, talk and act for themselves, and to be free and happy, but first to be wise and good.

SHELLEY professed to have little respect for the marriage relation. In a letter to a friend he says: "I am a young man, not of age, and have been married for a year to a woman younger than myself. Love seems inclined to stay in prison, and my only reason for putting him in chains, whilst convinced of the unholiness of the act, was a knowledge that, in the present state of society, if love is not thus villainously treated, she who is most loved will be treated worst by a misjudging world."

His marriage proved an unhappy one. Domestic discord ensued, which soon ended in separation and divorce. Circumstances ere long brought them together, and they were again united. But the heart, once estranged from the object of its affections, is ever afterward cold and passionless. A faint light may glimmer for a while on the altar, but the sacred fire is never again renewed. The urn itself is polluted, and breaks as it were from very coldness, refusing even to hold the ashes of its former love. After the separation, SHELLEY traveled on the continent with Mary Godwin, the daughter of William Godwin and Mary Wolstonecraft. On his return to England he learned that his wife had committed suicide. This event tinged with sorrow the remainder of his life.

It is thought that he endeavored to describe his feelings

at this occurrence in the portrait of the maniac in "Julian and Maddalo."

It is almost impossible to say to what extent SHELLEY is to blame for the causes which led this unhappy woman to seek refuge from her troubles in the grave. It is certain that she became imbued with his religious opinions, and was thus deprived of the only comfort that could possibly bring rest to her weary soul.

In a short time after this occurrence, he married Miss Godwin, and to her we must attribute the inspiration of some of his greatest poems. In 1818 he wrote his "Beatrice Cenci," and in 1819 his beautiful tribute to Keats.

SHELLEY was passionately fond of boating. There was no other amusement that afforded him so much pleasure. In July, 1822, he and a Mr. Williams sailed from Leghorn to Lerici in a boat of peculiar construction, requiring the most skilful management. The boat was upset in a storm, and their bodies were washed ashore. In SHELLEY'S pocket was found a copy of Keats' poem, "Lamia." The quarantine regulations of Tuscany required everything to be burnt that drifted to shore. In accordance with this custom, his remains were burned in the presence of Lord Byron, Leigh' Hunt, and Mr. Trelawney. A funeral pyre was made of the most precious materials, including frankincense, perfume, and wine. As the beautiful flame lifted its quivering light to heaven, it is said to have looked as though it contained the glassy essence of vitality.

His ashes were collected and deposited in the Protestant burial-ground in Rome, near the grave of Keats, where flowers ever bloom and breathe their perfume upon the air.

SHELLEY has been cited as an august example to those who aspire to universal knowledge. He was the most diligent of students. He read and studied at all times — at table, in bed, and while walking and riding. Out of the twenty-four hours he frequently read eighteen. It is said that he was unrivaled in the justness and extent of his observations on natural objects, and that he knew every plant by its name, and was familiar with all the productions of the earth.

It would be difficult to define his views of religion. Indeed, it would seem that he had no fixed or settled ideas of religion. In "Queen Mab" he speaks of a spirit of the universe and a co-eternal fairy of the earth. At one time he believed in the doctrine of a pre-existing state. On one occasion he met a ragged, bare-headed gypsy girl, about five or six years old, gathering shells. He ran up to her and exclaimed: "How much intellect is here, and what an occupation for one who once knew the whole circle of the sciences — who has forgotten them all, it is true, but who could certainly recollect them, though it is most probable she never will."

After propounding a number of questions to the little gypsy, which of course were unintelligible to her, he turned from her and said to a friend accompanying him, "Every true Platonist must be fond of children, for they are our masters in philosophy. The mind of a new-born child is not, as Locke says, a sheet of blank paper. On the contrary it is an Elzevir Plato, say rather an encyclopædia, comprising all that ever was or ever will be discovered."

Quite a number of similar stories are told illustrative of SHELLEY's faith in the doctrine of Pre-existence. It is said that one day he met a woman on Magdalen Bridge with a child in her arms. He immediately seized it, to the horror of the mother, who took him for a madman, and was fearful that he might throw it in the water. SHELLEY exclaimed, "Madam, will your baby tell us anything about Pre-existence?" On being assured that the child could not speak, he continued, "Worse and worse; but surely the babe can speak if he will, for he is only a few weeks old. He may perhaps fancy that he cannot, but that is a silly whim. He cannot have entirely forgotten the use of speech in so short a time. The thing is impossible."

We cannot take leave of SHELLEY without a few words in regard to his poetry.

He was perhaps the most perfect versifier in the language. His words seemed ever to come winged and obedient to his call. His lines to "An Indian Air," and his "Ode to the Skylark," are unequaled for the exquisite softness and delicacy of their rhythm and melody. They give "a very echo to the seat where Love is throned." Words fail to express sufficient admiration for the "Sensitive Plant." It seems that a touch would profane it. It is of this world, and yet not of this world. We have in it everything that is deliciously ravishing in romance and poetry. It is everywhere enameled with thoughts of gold. Passion seems to emanate from it as if from a shrine. It is like an exhalation from the most exquisite perfume that dies, as it were, from its very sweetness. All the inspiration at the command of genius, beauty, power, and passion, breathes and glows and burns around it, and we are as much impressed with its weird and inexplicable philosophy,

> "Where nothing is, but all things seem,
> And we the shadows of the dream,"

as with the delicious and entrancing music of its numbers. What could be finer than the description of the flowers that bloomed in the garden where the Sensitive Plant closed its fan-like leaves beneath the kisses of night?—

> "And the Naiad-like Lily of the vale,
> Whom youth makes so fair and passion so pale;
>
> And the Rose like a nymph to the bath addressed,
> Which unveiled the depth of her glowing breast,
> Till fold after fold to the fainting air
> The soul of her beauty and love lay bare."

The description of the Eve of this Eden, who "tended this garden fair," is even more passionately beautiful:

> "She had no companion of mortal race,
> But her tremulous breath and flushing face
> Told, while the morn kissed the sleep from her eyes,
> That her dreams were less slumber than Paradise.

> "As if some bright spirit, for her sweet sake,
> Had deserted Heaven while the stars were awake;
> As if yet around her he lingering were,
> Though the veil of daylight concealed him from her."

"Epipsychidion," next to the "Sensitive Plant," is the most strangely beautiful of all the author's productions. It is one of the most exquisite love-poems in the whole range of English literature. It is the very soul of passion and purity. There is not the slightest taint of indelicacy about it. There is nothing whatever in it that could tend to convey the impression of licentiousness or sensuality. It is confused in passion's golden purity.

> "Like a naked bride,
> Glowing at once with love and loveliness,
> Blushes and trembles at its own excess."

In a former part of this sketch we spoke of SHELLEY'S insane speculations upon the Christian religion. It is gratifying to know that as he advanced in life his faith became more and more weakened in the wretched philosophy which he endeavored to substitute for the divine precepts of our Saviour. Had he lived a few years longer, we do not doubt that his atheistical opinions would have been wholly discarded.

ANTONY AND CLEOPATRA.

ANTONY AND CLEOPATRA deservedly stands in the front rank of SHAKSPEARE'S Roman historical dramas. It is one of the most wonderful, varied, and magnificent of all his creations. There is an irregular grandeur about it that presents a striking contrast to the restrained and thoughtful emotions and passions delineated in "Coriolanus" and "Julius Cæsar." Critics unite in the opinion that it was written at a period when the author's mind was in the fulness of its power. Coleridge says: "The highest praise, or rather form of praise, of this play which I can offer in my own mind, is the doubt which the perusal always occasions in me whether ANTONY AND CLEOPATRA is not, in all exhibitions of a giant power, in its strength and vigor of maturity, a formidable rival of "Macbeth," "Lear," "Hamlet," and "Othello."

He places it in mental contrast with "Romeo and Juliet" "as the love of passion and appetite opposed to the love of affection and instinct."

There is little or no resemblance between Juliet and CLEOPATRA. The love of Juliet is the love of youth and innocence. It has all the warmth, and tenderness, and luxuriance of the climate in which she lived. The love of CLEOPATRA, on the contrary, is the love of a woman, as she herself says, who has passed her "salad days," and is no longer "green in judgment." It is a love that rages like the fury of a north wind. It is vehement, tumultuous, stormy. It has the strength and fierceness of the tiger in it. There is nothing crude and unripe about it. She ever struggles to increase and stimulate it, and to mingle with it all the cravings of a licentious and voluptuous nature.

The minuteness with which SHAKSPEARE has followed history in this play is truly wonderful. He has embraced in it almost every incident and person mentioned by Plutarch, and what is added has such an air of truth that we do not once think of doubting its reality. Hence SHAKSPEARE'S CLEOPATRA is the CLEOPATRA of history. In depicting her rare beauty and accomplishments, he is not unmindful of the dark shades of her nature. She regards human life and happiness as mere playthings. Murder and violence are not strangers to her any more than passion and lust. She is "the foul Egyptian" as well as the "great fairy" and "sweet queen." It is next to an impossibility to understand her character or to unravel it, if indeed it is not inexplicable. The more we study it, the more we are puzzled and bewildered. Every attempt to analyse it leads us into an interminable labyrinth of error and inconsistency. It may be because she is made up of inconsistencies. If she is consistent in anything it is in being inconsistent. There is a fascination about her that is irresistible. She displays a thousand graces and beauties at once, and a thousand faults and follies. It is impossible to tell what to admire most in her, or what most to detest. She seems to be as full of truth and honor as she is of fickleness and falsehood. At times she is more charming and witty than Beatrice, more tender and beautiful than Imogen, more passionate and enthusiastic than Juliet, more graceful and ethereal than Miranda, more poetic and imaginative than Viola, and more stately and dignified than Hermione. Then, again, she seems to be very far from anything of the kind. If she is unlike any one it is Octavia, who is of a dull and still conversation, who shows a body rather than a life, a statue rather than a breather.

CLEOPATRA is well called the "great fairy," "enchantress," "a most triumphant lady," "cockatrice," "serpent of old Nile," "cunning past man's thought," "a most wonderful piece of work," "the rare Egyptian," and "noble queen."

Every word she utters, every thought she expresses seems to belong wholly to her.

What a strange method she has of enforcing love when she says,

> "See where he is — who's with him — what he does.
> (I did not send you.) If you find him sad,
> Say I am dancing; if in mirth, report
> That I am sudden sick! Quick and return."

How thoroughly and completely she fills the idea of a wilful and capricious coquette, but a coquette unlike any other in the world's history. Enobarbus tells ANTONY, in speaking of the latter's departure for Rome, "CLEOPATRA, catching the least noise of this, dies instantly. I have seen her die twenty times upon far poorer moment."

The imagination is surfeited with the description of her charms. We need not be told of globed and gleaming limbs,—

> "For her own person
> It beggared all description. She did lie
> In her pavilion (cloth of gold of tissue)
> O'erpicturing that Venus where we see
> The fancy outwork nature.
> *   *   *   *   *
> Age cannot wither her, nor custom stale
> Her infinite variety. Other women cloy
> The appetites they feed, but she makes hungry
> Where most she satisfies: for vilest things
> Become themselves in her."

The charm by which she enslaved the passions of ANTONY, "the greatest soldier of the world," "the demi-Atlas of the earth," "the arm and burgonet of men," is admirably portrayed in the following. It is a wonderful description of the imperial and self-conscious power of woman's evil influence over the affections and passions of man.

> "That time — O time!
> I laughed him out of patience; and that night
> I laughed him into patience; and next morn,
> Ere the ninth hour, I drunk him to his bed;
> Then put my tires and mantles on, whilst
> I wore his sword Philippan."

SHAKSPEARE has endowed ANTONY with the noblest attributes. While we deplore the spell of "the enchantress" over him, we feel that he must be admired as "the garland of war," and that upon his sword should sit "laurel victory and smooth success."

His lasciviousness and illness did hatch ten thousand ills; but he is the ANTONY who fought at Philippi and at Modena, who slew Hirtius and Pansa, and endured famine, though "daintily brought up, with patience more than savages could suffer." He is the triple pillar of the world, the great Triumvir who would be "treble-sinewed hearted, breathed and fight maliciously," the ANTONY whom none but ANTONY could conquer. The scene in which his death is foreshadowed is what Hazlitt calls the finest piece of poetry in SHAKSPEARE. "The splendor of the imagery, the semblance of reality, the lofty range of picturesque objects hanging over the world, their evanescent nature, the total uncertainty of what is left behind, are just like the mouldering schemes of human greatness."

> " Sometime we see a cloud that's dragonish,
> A vapor sometime like a bear or lion,

> A towered citadel, a pendant rock,
> A forked mountain, or blue promontory
> With trees upon't, that nod unto the world
> And mock our eyes with air. Thou hast seen these signs:
> They are black vesper's pageants."

He was indeed a fit companion for CLEOPATRA; for who but one "with half the bulk of the world played as he pleased," could mate with her?

The influence she wielded over Cæsar and Pompey serves to heighten the power of her blandishments, and palliate the conduct of him who "madly threw a world away."

Cæsar's marriage with her was merely nominal, but it is stated that he lived openly with her in his palace under the eyes of his legitimate wife.

ANTONY speaks of CLEOPATRA as being "half blasted ere he knew her," and as finding her "a morsel cold upon dead Cæsar's trencher," and as a fragment of Cneius Pompey's, but history hardly confirms the story of her libertinism with Pompey.

It is said to be inconsistent with the character of the man whom Cicero describes as *hominum castum et severum et integrum et gravem.*

One of the finest scenes in the play is where the Egyptian Circe calls Charmian to give her "drink of mandagora," that she may "sleep out this great gap of time while ANTONY is away." It is here that she says,

> "He's speaking now
> Or murmuring, 'Where's my serpent of old Nile?'
> For so he calls me. Now I feed myself
> With most delicious poison. Think on me
> That am with Phœbus' amorous pinches black,
> And wrinkled deep in time."

ANTONY sends her, in this part of the play, a pearl, with

a message that he will piece her opulent throne with kingdoms, and all the East shall call her mistress.

CLEOPATRA's warmth of affection is admirably contrasted with her perverseness and petulance in the scene where she receives a messenger from Rome with the tidings of ANTONY's marriage:

> "ANTONY's dead!
> If thou say so, villain, thou killest thy mistress.
> But well and free,
> If thou so yield him, there is gold, and here
> My bluest veins to kiss; a hand that kings
> Have lipped, and trembled kissing."

The pride and beauty of high rank are here grandly displayed. It seems almost a pity to take this poetic gem from its setting.

The entire scene should be read in order to fully appreciate its wonderful variety of imagery and gorgeousness of coloring. In no other part of the play does she seem to fuse together so much majesty and spirit, and talent, tact and wit, pride and generosity, petulance and wilfulness, caprice and fickleness.

CLEOPATRA's peculiar qualities are displayed in everything she does, even in the choice of her attendants. Charmian and Iris have a recklessness and daring, a wantonness and levity, that seem especially adapted for ministering to the wants and pleasures of such a queen. A woman like Charmian, who wished to be married to three kings in an afternoon, and to widow them all and have a child at fifty to whom Herod of Jewry might do homage, would hardly suit for the companionship of any one else but CLEOPATRA.

The grandeur of CLEOPATRA's death does much to relieve her unpardonable crimes, and to soften the dark traits of her character. She preserved her majesty and dignity to the last. She would be seen even in death only as a queen, crown and all. Her command is: "Go fetch my best attires; I am again for Cydnus to meet MARC ANTONY."

She who boasted in the presence of "the case of that huge spirit"—

> "It were for me
> To throw my sceptre at the injurious gods,
> To tell them that this world did equal theirs,
> Till they had stolen our jewel,"

might indeed be said to look in deathlike sleep as

> "She would catch another ANTONY
> In her strong toil of grace."

CYMBELINE.

CYMBELINE is the most romantic and imaginative of all SHAKSPEARE's plays. It seems to give birth to every wave of thought, of feeling and reflection. Every excellence in woman is delineated in the character of the heroine, Imogen. She is the very soul of purity, of honor and goodness. Every word she utters sounds like a sweet note of music from some undiscovered orb of song. Her intellect is almost as wonderful as her beauty, and her beauty is the most perfect dream of luxuriant loveliness. There is nothing vain, or haughty, or selfish about her. She is as peerless in the innate delicacy and majesty of her charms as a goddess. She moves through an atmosphere of corruption and deceit like a breath of summer, a glimpse of sunshine. She has the deepest and most exquisite sensibilities and the purest and loftiest affections. She combines in herself all the grace and tenderness and innocence and simplicity of youth, and all the strength and firmness and constancy of mature womanhood.

The plot of CYMBELINE is derived from various sources. SHAKSPEARE found in Hollingshead's *Chronicles of England and Scotland* some of the material of the play, including the names of CYMBELINE and his sons, together with some account of the King's reign, and the tribute demanded by the Romans. It is said that he also derived the beautiful name of Imogen from the same source, and that in the old black-letter it is scarcely distinguished from Innogen, the wife of Brute, King of Britain. The story of the discovery of the mole upon Imogen's breast is taken either from Boccaccio's beautiful novel of "Zeneura" in the Decameron, or from a French romance entitled *De La Violette*, first published in the thirteenth century.

The hero of *La Violette* is Gerard de Nevers, called the false Paridel of French romance. He is described as being young and handsome, and graced with many accomplishments. He obtains by stealth the knowledge of a secret mark upon the breast of the heroine.

> "Et vit sur sa destre mamele,
> . Une violete novele,
> Ynde parut sous la char blanche."

The above lines, Verplanc says, bear some resemblance to the description of the same incident in CYMBELINE; but adds, it is probable the English poet never read the story, and what seems to be an adaptation should be regarded only as a remarkable coincidence.

Collier, in his "Shakspeare's Library," gives an account of a French miracle-play, published in 1639, which contains some of the incidents of CYMBELINE, the wager on the chastity of the heroine, her flight in the disguise of a page, the proof of her innocence, and her final restoration to her husband. Mr. Collier says that the French play contains two circumstances introduced into CYMBELINE not found in any other version of the story, viz., the method of assailing the heroine's virtue by exciting her anger and jealousy, and the boast of one of the characters that "if he were allowed the opportunity of speaking to her but twice he should be able to accomplish his design."

SHAKSPEARE was doubtless acquainted with this play, but it is evident that he made use of Boccaccio's novel.

He was doubtless sufficiently versed in the Italian to read it in the original. We can imagine the impression Boccaccio's charming story made upon his mind. It is the most exquisite creation in the Decameron. The Griseldis will not begin to compare with it. It is even more fascinating than the "Giletta di Narbonna." Each and all the incidents are related with singular sweetness, and power, and beauty and clearness. We deeply sympathise with the trials and sufferings, the long and patient wanderings of the fair Zeneura, and rejoice at the punishment of the fiend who boasted, "Woman only is pure who has never been asked, or she who herself has asked and been refused."

But beautiful as is Boccaccio's story, Zeneura cannot be compared with Imogen. We see in the former only a rugged outline of the depths and soundings of the human passions, of the delicate and tender and confiding loveliness of the soul so wonderfully and eloquently portrayed in the latter. There are so many beauties in Imogen's character that it is almost impossible to analyse them or describe them.

In the parting scene in the first act we have the following inimitable description of unselfish love:

"Nay, stay a little.
Were you but riding forth to air yourself,
Such parting were too petty. Look here, love:
This diamond ring was my mother's; take it, heart,
But keep it till you woo another wife,
When Imogen is dead."

How deeply she feels the reproaches of her father against her husband when she says,

"There cannot be a pinch in death
More sharp than this!"

She is compelled to submit to the unexampled tyranny of "a father governed by a step-dame hourly coining plots," and to the serpent-like approaches of the "yellow Iachimo," who is destitute of any redeeming traits whatever. This fiend, armed with audacity from head to foot, like Iago, only lives to assail virtue and destroy happiness. His moral constitution is utterly incapable of digesting anything but poison. And yet he is introduced to IMOGEN as "one of the noblest note," as one to whom her husband is "most infinitely tied." When this base slanderer insinuates that Posthumus is a renegade from her bed, and indulges in "vaulting variable ramps" at her expense, she believes nothing in haste, and offers no other reproach than

"My Lord, I fear, has forgotten Britain."

The more we study her the more we love and admire her. She ever presents the most complete and perfect idea of womanhood. Even in the most trying scenes she never loses her self-possession. SHAKSPEARE has nowhere given a wider scope to his imagination than in the delineation of her character. And yet none of his heroines are more lifelike and natural. She charms all who behold her. Even in her male attire we are constantly impressed with the inborn delicacy and refinement and purity of her principles. She is indeed the embodiment of love and innocence, the sweetest, fairest lily. No wonder Guiderius exclaims when seeing her disguised as a page, "Were you a woman, youth, I should woo hard but be your groom, in honesty," and that Lucius, the Roman General, should call her "the page, so kind, so duteous, diligent."

Perhaps the most luxurious display of the personal charms of woman in SHAKSPEARE is the description of Imogen in the sleeping scene. It is unequaled for the gorgeous richness of its coloring, and the variety and splendor of its imagery.

"The crickets sing, and man's o'erlabor'd sense
Repairs itself by rest; our Tarquin thus

> Did softly press the rushes, ere he 'waken'd
> The chastity he wounded.— Cytherea,
> How bravely thou becom'st thy bed! fresh lily,
> And whiter than the sheets! that I might touch!
> But kiss, one kiss! rubies unparagon'd!
> How dearly they do't! 'Tis her breathing that
> Perfumes the chamber thus; the flame o' the taper
> Bows toward her, and would underpeep her lids
> To see th' inclosed lights now canopied
> Under these windows, white and azure, lac'd
> With blue of heaven's own tinct; on her left breast
> A mole cinque-spotted like the crimson drops
> I' the bottom of a cowslip."

The words in which she mourns the loss of her bracelet, which Iachimo had stolen for the purpose of convincing her husband of her infidelity, are beautiful beyond description :

> "Go, bid my woman
> Search for a jewel that too casually
> Hath left my arm. It was thy master's: 'shrew me,
> If I would lose it for a revenue
> Of any king in Europe. I do think
> I saw't this morning; confident I am
> Last night 'twas on mine arm. I kiss'd it.
> I hope it has not gone to tell my lord
> That I kiss aught but he."

It has been said that " our consciousness that the bracelet is really gone to bear false witness against her, adds an inexpressibly touching effect to the simplicity and tenderness of the sentiment."

In studying this play it is difficult to believe that Posthumus deserves forgiveness. His wager about his wife's chastity and his readiness to believe her guilty, to say nothing of his rashness in pursuing his revenge, one would think could scarcely excite any other feeling than that of contempt. But then, on the other hand, we must not forget Imogen's unconquerable love for him, and that she herself forgave him, and that he is described as one who sat among men like a descended god, with an honor about him more than mortal seeming.

HAMLET.

IN discussing, some years ago, with a friend, the merits of Edwin Booth's performance of HAMLET, he urged as an objectionable feature in Booth's delineation of the character that he did his utmost to convey the impression that HAMLET'S madness was not real but only feigned. My friend argued that there was nothing in the play to warrant such a conclusion. He said it was certainly SHAKSPEARE'S intention to define clearly and unmistakably one of the most palpable, as well as one of the most interesting phases of insanity, and that we could not assign any other reason than madness for his wild and irregular disposition, and pointless and purposeless conduct.

I attempted to refute this theory by suggesting that any refined and cultivated nature would have acted just as HAMLET did, if surrounded by the same circumstances. I said that, in order to understand fully the secret workings of HAMLET'S conscience, we must look upon him as a being compounded, like other men, with a goodly share of both the faults and virtues of humanity, and that we must remember the horror of his situation, the supernatural visitation of his father's spirit in arms, and the awful command it gave him "not to let the royal bed of Denmark be a couch for luxury and damned incest." These suggestions were met by a eulogy upon the character of Ophelia. She was described as the most perfect incarnation of virtue, of gentleness and innocence. She was compared "to the rose of May — O flower too soon faded?"— to the summer cloud, the snow-flake, the voice of silvery fountains, the charm of earliest birds, and to all that is lovely and lovable in the worlds of reality and imagination.

Being unable to recall any considerable portion of the text by which I hoped to sustain the position that HAMLET'S madness was assumed, I was at length silenced with the exclamation that no one but a brute or a madman "loosed out of hell," could outrage the exquisite sensibilities of a woman constituted like Ophelia, by ordering her to a nunnery, asking her if she would be a breeder of sinners, and saying, "God hath given you one face, and you give yourselves another; you jig, you amble, and you lisp, and nickname God's creatures, and make your wantonness your ignorance."

I am free to confess that I was so impressed with this conversation that I determined immediately to study the play with the greatest care, and to read everything that I could procure in relation to it, with a view of settling definitely and forever in my mind this perplexing feature in the character of this darling of the English stage — this prince courtier, scholar and gentleman, whose subtle arguments and philosophical meditations penetrate into the profoundest recesses of the soul. My study and researches have been rewarded with the most fixed and settled convictions that HAMLET was not mad — neither partially nor wholly — and that SHAKSPEARE never intended to convey the idea of madness any further than to surround the play with an air of mystery for the purpose of heightening its beauty and sublimity.

In the earliest edition of HAMLET, that of 1603, we find that SHAKSPEARE made the description of HAMLET'S madness much stronger than he did in the amended copy. The edition of 1608 was doubtless an imperfect copy of the first conception of the poet. The later edition was such an improvement on the first that the date of it has generally been regarded as the period that marks the birth of that thoughtful philosophy so wonderfully portrayed in all the carefully-elaborated works of the author.

In the first copy the King speaks of HAMLET as having "lost the very heart of all his sense," while in the amended one he speaks of him simply as being "put from the understanding of himself."

In the first copy, Polonius speaks of his madness changing by continuance "into this frenzy which now possesses him." In the revised copy we have "a fast, a watch, a weakness, a lightness, and a madness."

Charles Knight, one of the most indefatigable of Shakspearean scholars, remarks that the reason of this change is that "SHAKSPEARE did not, either in his first sketch or his amended copy, intend his audience to believe that HAMLET was essentially mad, and he removed, therefore, the strong expressions which might encourage that belief."

Dr. Johnson thought HAMLET'S madness feigned, but was silly enough to add that it "excited much mirth."

Coleridge has, perhaps, shown a more critical appreciation of HAMLET than any of the other modern Shakspearean scholars (unless, indeed, we except some of the German critics, Lessing and Schlegel for instance), takes the position that HAMLET'S wildness is but half false, that he plays that subtle trick of pretending to act only when he is very near really being what he acts. Coleridge, however, reconciles HAMLET'S sanity in the scene with Ophelia on the ground that "the Prince perceived, from the strange and forced manner of Ophelia, that the sweet girl was not acting a part of her own, but was a decoy, and his after speeches were not so much directed to her as to the spies and listeners."

The idea that HAMLET's wildness was but half false doubtless formed the ground-work for the beautiful and ingenious theory of Henry Hudson, viz., that "HAMLET's madness is neither real nor affected, but is a sort of natural and spontaneous imitation of madness; the triumph of his reason over passion naturally expressing itself in the tokens of insanity, just as the agonies of despair naturally vent themselves in flashes of mirth."

Dr. John Connoly, in a little work entitled "A Study of Hamlet," sustains the theory of HAMLET's madness with considerable zeal, on the ground that the Prince could not have misled Ophelia, who was accustomed to read his inmost thoughts. Dr. Kellogg, a physician to the State lunatic asylum of New York, takes the same position, and says, "Ophelia was no incompetent judge. The lynx-eyed vigilance of woman's love could not be deceived, and she has read correctly the riddle which has so perplexed all Shakspearean critics."

Dr. Ray in his work on Medical Jurisprudence, also maintains the same view; but surely these physicians, who claim to have given so much study to the pathology of the mind, ought not to forget that chronic mania is very easily feigned, and often feigned successfully. Dr. Bucknill relates an instance of a gentleman who kept up the practice of insanity for more than two years before he broke down in his part, and of another who kept up the practice much longer. I have myself observed cases where the ablest physicians were unable to detect the imposture. Indeed, the task is often as difficult as the detection of partial idealiation insanity, where the patient is suspicious and tries to hide it.

The theory of HAMLET's madness is very popular with

the French school of critics. M. Villemain, in a late work, has quite settled it to his entire satisfaction; but of all critics of SHAKSPEARE, the French have shown themselves the most incompetent and unappreciative. Those who have undertaken to translate his plays into French, without a single exception performed their work most abominably. The story of the Frenchman translating the phrase "Frailty, thy name is woman," into "Frailty *is* the name of a woman," is scarcely an exaggeration.

It has been said that HAMLET'S conduct cannot be accounted for solely on the ground of the absorbing and overwhelming influence of the one paramount thought which renders hopeless and ,worthless all that formerly occupied his affections, from the fact that it is not directly supported by the text, though worthy of the feeling and conception of the poet. Whether worthy or not, I can but believe that HAMLET'S purpose of avenging his father's murder is the chief business of the play. It seems to have occupied HAMLET's thoughts to the exclusion of "all trivial fond records, all saws of books, all forms, all pressures past." He considers nothing else half so deeply. Because he should have doubts and misgivings, and ask if the ghost is an honest ghost, and be deeply affected at Ophelia's too confiding obedience to her father, there is no reason to believe that there is anything unnatural or inconsistent in it. The play would not be what it is if HAMLET had but one thought and object. The truth is, SHAKSPEARE did not intend to portray HAMLET unlike the rest of the human family, but to give us a kind of idealised picture of humanity; not the portrait of an individual character, but of a universal nature, a nature that pervades all classes of society; and this alone is the cause of a want of unanimity of opinion concerning the purpose of the author. If there were no complexity about the play we could see through it at a glance, and would cast it aside, caring nothing whatever about it.

It is hardly necessary to say anything further in palliation of HAMLET's treatment of Ophelia; but those who have had the good fortune to witness Booth's personation of HAMLET cannot fail to have observed the painful expression of his countenance when upbraiding her. With brow slightly knit and the lower lip tightly compressed, and "pale as his shirt," he endeavors, almost as if by a superhuman effort, to conceal the pain it gives him; but when his face is turned from her, the indescribable agony of his soul is made wonderfully apparent in the fearful writhings of his countenance. We almost hear

> "A sigh so piteous and profound
> That it did seem to shatter all his bulk,
> And end his being."

If HAMLET wished the command of the ghost to live within the book and volume of his brain, and to avenge

> "Such an act,
> That blurs the grace and blush of modesty;
> Calls virtue hypocrite; takes off the rose
> From the fair forehead of innocent love,
> And sets a blister there; makes marriage vows
> As false as dicers' oaths,"

surely Ophelia should be the last person in the world to possess a knowledge of the means by which he hoped to accomplish it. He could not help "being cruel in order to be kind." Moreover, HAMLET's harshness was aimed not so much at her as at her sex. The plague he gave her as a dowry, "Be thou as chaste as ice, as pure as snow, thou canst not escape calumny," is the severest speech he makes directly to her.

When HAMLET first conceived the idea of putting an antic disposition on, his next thought was how to conceal it, and for this reason he treated the ghost with pretended levity, in such speeches as

> "Ha, ha, boy! says't thou so? art thou there, true penny?
> Come on — you hear this fellow in the cellarage —
> Consent to swear!"

And —

> "Well said, old mole! can't work in the earth so fast,
> A worthy pioneer."

Hence his swearing Horatio and Marcellus to secrecy —

> "That you at such times seeing me never shall,
> With arms encumbered thus, or this, head shake,
> Or, by pronouncing of some doubtful phrase,
> As, 'Well, well, we knew'— or, 'We could an if we would '—
>   or, 'if we list'— or,
> 'There be an if they might,'
> Or such ambiguous giving out to note
> That you know aught of me,— this not to do,
> So grace and mercy at your most need help you.
> Swear!"

HAMLET, the reader will observe, evaded the curiosity of his friends as best he could. The speech, "There's ne'er a villain in all Denmark," was followed by "But he's an arrant knave." Why should he trust them? His confidence in all earthly things was shaken. He had heard "the secrets of the prison-house," "the eternal blazon that must not be to ears of flesh and blood." It was fitting that he should beg them to overmaster their curiosity as best they could, and shake hands and part "without more circumstance at all." "The time was out of joint," and he alone was called upon "to set it right."

But, alas! the tragical end that awaited him and all its accompanying horrors. The meditative and thoughtful philosophy of his disposition unfitted him for the awful duty enjoined upon him by the voice from the unseen world. It was an act of vengeance against the laws of the land, to be justified only in the court of his own conscience, and by the philosophy, "There's nothing good or bad, but thinking makes it so;" but he unhesitatingly and unshrinkingly devoted his life to the sacrifice.

DAVID GARRICK.

DAVID GARRICK was born at Hereford, in 1716. He lived during one of the most interesting periods in the history of English literature. His father was a captain in the English army, but settled at Litchfield on half-pay, with the hope of being able to support his family. All his efforts in this direction were fruitless. He experienced the severest trials of poverty. He was compelled to join his regiment again in 1731, in order to relieve distress. His wife, poor dear, faithful creature, broken in health and spirits, undertook the care of a family of seven children. We cannot attempt to describe her suffering during the absence of her husband. She loved him with a devotion not of earth, but of some purer realm. In the midst of trouble and sickness and distress, she ever looked forward to a bright and happy future, when no cloud should darken the threshold of her happy home. The words of comfort she sent to the absent husband and father unlock all the portals of the heart capable of being moved by words of sympathy and love. "I must tell my dear life and soul," she writes, in a letter breathing the tenderest vow of affection, and which a reviewer says reads like a bit of Thackeray or Sterne, "that I am not able to live any longer without him, for I grow very jealous. But in the midst of all this I do not blame my dear. I have very sad dreams for you, but I have the pleasure when I am up to think were I with you, how tender my dear would be to me — nay, was when I was with you last. Oh, that I had you in my arms! I would tell my dear life how much I am his."

How slowly the time passed! Only two years were gone — three more were to elapse before they were to be together again. O cruel fate! why is it that the records of loved and loving hearts are so often written in tears and blood? The husband returned at last, but only to die in the arms of his fond and faithful wife. It is almost unnecessary to add that in less than one year her troubled soul too was at rest.

In early youth GARRICK displayed extraordinary talent for acting. When eleven years of age he acted in a play entitled "The Recruiting Officer," and received no little applause from a select audience. In 1728 he went to Lisbon to visit a wealthy uncle, and while at his house often amused dinner parties by the recitation of poems and speeches. He would then have adopted the profession of an actor, but his family had a great prejudice against the stage, and his kind and gentle and affectionate disposition would not allow him to do aught that would add to their displeasure.

At eighteen he was one of the three pupils at Dr. Johnson's "Academy." A few years afterward he went to London in company with his teacher. The latter described their pecuniary condition by saying that one had but two-pence half-penny in his pocket, and the other three half-pence in his. Johnson doubtless endeavored to make sport of their condition, but it is certain that their means were indeed limited.

GARRICK tried his fortune as a wine merchant, with indifferent success. Foote, the author of the popular farce on Taste, and one of the wittiest as well as one of the meanest of men, used to say that he recollected GARRICK calling himself a wine merchant with but three quarts of vinegar in his cellar.

GARRICK attended the theatres of London constantly, and in 1740 had made some reputation as a dramatic critic and as an elocutionist. In 1741 he made his first appearance as an actor at Ipswich. A few months later he played Richard III. before a London audience. His reputation was at once secured. His fame spread rapidly throughout the country. The *beau monde* of London vied with one another in doing him homage. He was everywhere admired and praised. He was dined, wined and feasted, not only by people of fashion, but by the greatest authors, lawyers and statesmen. He won the friendship of Burke, of Pitt, and of Lyttleton, of Reynolds and Goldsmith. Leonidas Glover called to see him every day. Even the bard of Twickenham, now old and feeble and ill in health, left his home to see him. The London press teemed with the most enthusiastic eulogies upon his wonderful gifts. The *Post* declared him to be the most extraordinary man ever known. The history of the stage was searched in vain for a parallel. He had totally eclipsed the fame of Booth, and Quin, and Betterton. The Duke of Argyle could not find language extravagant enough to praise him. The cynical Walpole said that he was the greatest actor that ever lived, either in tragedy or comedy. Even Bishop Newton wrote to him, "I have seen your Richard, Chamont, Bayes, and Lear. I never saw four actors more different from one another than you are from yourself." Macklin, who disliked him, and who struggled to rival him, thus spoke of his Lear, "The curse was particularly grand. It seemed to electrify the audience with horror. The words 'Kill! kill! kill!' echoed all the revenge of a frantic king." Everything he played added to his reputation. There was something almost idolatrous about the honors shown him.

He was looked upon "less with admiration than wonder." Though small in stature, he awed every one who beheld him with the majesty of his appearance. Johnson, who had no appreciation whatever of acting, at one time pretended to dislike him, but would never allow any one else to speak ill of him. When GARRICK suggested some changes in the tragedy of "Irene," "Sir," said Johnson, "the fellow wants me to make Mahomet run mad, that he may have an opportunity of tossing his head and kicking his heels." At another time he spoke of him "as a fellow who claps a hump on his back and a lump on his leg, and cries, 'I am Richard III.'" Even Boswell confesses that Johnson was jealous of the fame of GARRICK, and that it was incomprehensible to him that an actor's art should be esteemed so highly. Johnson, however, was either too conscientious, or had too high a regard for the opinion of others, not to acknowledge him the greatest actor he had ever seen.

But notwithstanding the many epithets Johnson applied to GARRICK, he offered to write his life, wept the bitterest tears at his funeral, and afterwards spoke of his death as an "event that had eclipsed the gaiety of nations." He took leave of the stage in 1776, in the part of Don Felix, in the comedy of "Wonder." He was greeted by a distinguished and an enthusiastic audience. His farewell address was eloquent and affecting in the extreme, and moved his hearers to tears. He died in 1779, and was buried in Westminster Abbey, near the monument of Shakspeare.

Few persons have been more distinguished for domestic and social virtues than this great actor. He was kind, and gentle, and charitable. He was on terms of intimacy with nearly all the great men of his time. He was ever ready to assist, both with his purse and with his sympathy, every deserving person who applied to him. There was but one thing about him that we do not love to think of. We allude to his unworthy attachment to the beautiful but frail Peg Woffington. She was a fine actress, and possessed the rarest gifts for the appreciation of excellence and merit in others. She was a brilliant talker, and charmed all who drew near her with her quick, ready wit, and sparkling humor. She could portray a fine lady to perfection. In such characters as Millamant and Lady Townley she reigned without a rival. She sprang from the lowest dregs of society. She had been actually picked up out of the streets of Dublin, crying "half-penny salads." She has been described as a dazzling creature, with a head of beautiful form, perched like a bird upon a throat massive, yet shapely, and smooth as a column of alabaster, with dark eyes full of fire and tenderness, a delicious mouth with a hundred varying expressions, and that marvelous faculty of giving beauty alike to love or scorn, a sneer or a smile. But with all her graces of mind and person, she lacked constancy and fidelity. She professed to care only for the society of gentlemen, and often said that women talked of nothing but silks and scandal. She is said to have played the character of Sir Harry Wildair even better than GARRICK. The latter refused to compete with her in it, and abandoned the part wholly to her. On one occasion she was so pleased with the applause she received in this character, that she ran from the stage into the green-room, and exclaimed, "By Jove! I believe one-half the audience think I am a man." To which Quin replied, " Madam, the other half, then, have the best reason of knowing to the contrary."

GARRICK at one time thought of marrying her, but his better nature triumphed over this folly.

He was a singularly pure-hearted man, a profound scholar, and was versed in an infinite variety of knowledge, both of a literary and scientific character. All his contributions to literature, his poems, his verses, his prologues, his farces, and his dramatic criticisms, were written with more than average ability. Many of his epigrams, such as the one upon Goldsmith, will live as long as the language is spoken. He was wholly free from envy and jealousy. No language is sufficiently strong to describe his affection for his wife. She has herself said that he was more of a lover to her than a husband. Her devotion to him was almost unequaled. During the thirty years of their married life they were never one day apart. She was one of the most beautiful and accomplished women of her time.

She came from Vienna. She had been a dancer in the theatre. She brought letters of recommendation from the Empress Theresa, who thought her too beautiful to remain near the court of Francis I. In crossing the ocean in a ship from Helvoet to Harwich, she was dressed in male attire, and was taken for a young German Baron. During the voyage her conduct was modest and becoming. Indeed, it could not be otherwise, for, like Shakspeare's Rosalind, she had "no hose and doublet in her disposition." Her name was Eva Maria Veigel, and her friends called her "the beautiful Violette." She had little difficulty in winning her way into fashionable society with her virtue, grace, beauty, naiveté, and brilliant accomplishments. The Countess of Burlington took her to live with her, and gave her on the occasion of her marriage a dowry of £5,000.

Foote, who scarcely ever spoke well of any one, wrote to GARRICK in 1776: —

"It has been my misfortune not to know Mrs. GARRICK, but from what I have seen and all I have heard, you will have more to regret when either she or you die, than any man in the kingdom."

Wilkes called her the "first woman in England," and Churchill "the most agreeable one." Gibbon said that she possessed a secret more valuable than the philosopher's stone, that of gaining the hearts of all those who had the happiness of knowing her.

Hogarth painted their pictures in 1772, just two years after their marriage. It is one of the most beautiful, life-like, and interesting of the author's productions. Even the ordinary engraving taken from it has a delicacy, a freshness, and a beauty which we seldom see in the most carefully elaborated works of art.

We look at it involuntarily with the devotion of an enthusiast. There is something about it that speaks at once to the heart, to the feelings, and to the understanding. The spirit of truth, of consciousness, and beauty breathes around it.

This picture is known to every one. It portrays GARRICK in the act of composition. His countenance displays the deepest thought. His Violette, the best and truest of wives, is just behind him, ready to steal the pen from his hand, She is weary of his being "lost in thought — wrapt withal." She has the utmost confidence in his genius, and seems to feel that he has written enough to immortalise him, and that it is time for the inspiration to be dispelled, that she may tell him with love's own voice how dear he is to her.

Mrs. GARRICK survived her husband forty-three years. For more than a quarter of a century she would not allow any one to enter the sacred precincts of his darkened room. She died in 1822, loved and honored to the last. After such devotion, we need not wonder that every one who knew them was struck with the beautiful oneness of their lives.

Thackeray,

with a glance at vanity fair.

The leading magazines and periodicals of Europe and of this country have within the last few years been filled with essays and criticisms upon the life and genius of Thackeray. One class of his admirers proclaim him to be the greatest novelist who ever lived, and another the greatest humorist and satirist. As a critic and essayist he has been placed above Goldsmith, Macaulay, Carlyle, and Hazlitt. His poetry is said to be as good as Pope's and Beranger's, and better than Suckling's, or Pryor's, or Gay's, or Thomson's, or Southey's. The "Chronicle of the Drum," "The Cane-Bottomed Chair," and the ballad of "Bouillabaisse," go the rounds of the press as if written but yesterday. His epigrams and witty repartees speak volumes of sentiment. Not a few of his novels have passed into history.

The characters in "Vanity Fair," in "Pendennis," in the "Virginians," in "Esmond," and in the "Newcomes," are not only distinct and palpable creations, but are discussed and talked about like living human beings of flesh and blood.

Nearly everything he has written is tremulous with thought and emotion. He seems ever to display the keenest perception of truth, of beauty, and wisdom. His tenacious and penetrating intellect, his depths of sympathy and consciousness, his mingled gayety and earnestness of sentiment, and his subtle attractiveness of manner, are not surpassed by Scott, or Bulwer, or Dickens. He began his literary career at Cambridge, in 1829, by editing a series of papers called "The Snob; a Literary and Scientific Journal." In these papers he made some attempt at wit and humor, by committing droll errors in orthography and by aggrandising insignificant things. He soon became a contributor to the London press and to *Fraser's Magazine.* He wrote for the latter "Fitzboodle's Confessions," the "Fatal Boots," and the "Hoggarty Diamond." These efforts displayed talent of no common order, but attracted very little attention. He struggled almost ineffectually through weary years of obscurity, of neglect, and hardship, before he derived any reputation or profit from his labors. His greatest work, VANITY FAIR, had been rejected by several magazines, and he was compelled to publish it in monthly numbers after the fashion of Dickens' stories. Its success was at first doubted, but before it was completed he became known as one of the ablest writers of his time. VANITY FAIR presents a dreary picture of life, but, for aught we know, a true one. The characters that figure in it are drawn, not from the imagination, but from observation and experience. It is a pity that such villains as Lord Steyne exist in the world, but certainly the author is entitled to much credit for portraying them. We have met in real life an exact prototype of the weak and dissipated Captain Crawley, and have derived no little satisfaction from the manner in which we have been taught to regard him. The resemblance is carried so far that he never wrote home in his life except when he wanted money, and then his letters were full of dashes and bad grammar, and doubtless he spelled 'beseech' with an *a*, and 'earliest' without one. We do not know whether or not he is capable of exhibiting the same kind of courage that Captain Crawley did in the encounter with Lord Steyne, but we are quite sure that he is mean enough to accept favors from one who had sought to ruin him. The good-natured and reckless spendthrift, George Osborne, is a perfectly natural creation. So is also the vain and fat Joseph Sedley. The power, beauty, and interest of the story, however, cluster around the heroine, Becky Sharp. She is the most original, wonderful, and varied of all the author's creations. She is a perfect type of a class of bold, ambitious, cunning, intriguing, and selfish women. All the other characters in the book, wonderfully natural and life-like as they are, become, when brought in contact with her, but supernumerary beings, or, as it were, mere auxiliaries for the purpose of aiding in the development of the circumstances by which she is surrounded. She is constantly presenting some new phase in humanity, or illustrating some great lesson in moral and ethical philosophy. Whenever "she made a little circle for herself with incredible toils and labor, somebody came and swept it down rudely, and she had all her work to begin over again." All her powers of fascination, her artful appeals for sympathy, her exclamation, "Poor little me!" her wit, her beauty, her grace, ease and abandon, her archness and simplicity of manner, and girlish lightness of sentiment, fail to soften the dark shades of her character, or make us wish for her a better fate. She neglects her child, and lives only for the gratification of the meanest and lowest desires. She sells her virtue without even having the excuse of love or passion. THACKERAY was in his element when he conceived and portrayed her. He has done nothing else half so well. With all our admiration for his genius, we must confess that he delineates the character of a depraved being a thousand times better than he does that of a good one.

He has a terrible insight into the hearts of frivolous and intriguing women. He is almost enthusiastic in his descriptions of their base and ignoble passions. He not only describes their meanness, their spitefulness, their jealousy, and their selfishness, with painful minuteness, but actually rips them to pieces. It is believed that he could not portray a good woman at all. He attempted it in Ethel Newcome and in Amelia Sedley, two of his most prominent characters, and utterly failed. He made one a flirt and the other a fool. He has not escaped censure for such sermons as the following in VANITY FAIR and the "Newcomes" : —

"I know few things more affecting than that timorous debasement and self-humiliation of a woman. How she owns it is she and not the man who is guilty! How she takes all the faults on her side! How she courts in a manner punishment for the wrongs which she has not committed, and persists in shielding the real culprit. It is those who injure women who get the most kindness from them. They are born timid and tyrants, and maltreat those who are humblest before them."

"To coax, to flatter and befool some one is every woman's business; she is none if she declines this office. But men are not provided with such powers of humbug or endurance. They perish and pine away miserably when bored, or they shrink off to the club or public-house for comfort."

The closing scenes in VANITY FAIR, in which Becky Sharp's vagabond career is described, are beyond all question the finest in the book. THACKERAY was evidently a man of the world — an observer rather than a philosopher. He studied men and things more than he did books, or else he could not have pictured so vividly Joseph Sedley, creaking and puffing up the stairs which led above the rooms occupied by gamblers, small tradesmen, peddlers, and Bohemian vaulters and tumblers, "to where Becky had found a little nest, as dirty a little refuge as ever beauty lay hid in." The scene where the Dutch student, with the whitey-brown ringlets and large finger-ring, is bawling at the key-hole, while the gentleman from Bengal is approaching, is inimitable. Becky opens the door to see who is coming, and in an instant puts a rouge-pot, a brandy-bottle, and a plate of broken meat into the bed, gives a smooth to her hair, and lets in her visitor. Poor Joseph deserved to be wheedled by a woman who could sit upon a brandy-bottle, and play the coquette with rouge up to her eye-lids and a handkerchief of torn and faded lace. "She never was Lady Crawley, though she continued so to call herself."

But we close the book. If the author has not portrayed life as it ought to be, he has painted it as it really is. The lesson inculcated by exhibiting the awful and fearful consequences of placing the moral in subordination to the intellectual being, cannot easily be forgotten.

All's Well that Ends Well.

This play was originally called "Love's Labor Won." It is not known why or by whom the title was changed. Meares, a contemporary of SHAKSPEARE, speaks of "Love's Labor Won" as being among the best of SHAKSPEARE's comedies. He doubtless alludes to this play, for there is no other of the author's dramas to which the title is applicable. Moreover, there are several passages in the text in which allusions are made to its original name. In the fifth act Helena says to Bertram: —

> "This is done;
> Will you be mine now — you are doubly won?"

And again we have —

> "The King's a beggar, now the play is done;
> All is well ended if this suit be won."

Coleridge describes this drama as the counterpart of "Love's Labor Lost," and expresses the opinion that it was written at two different and distant periods of the poet's life, and points out two distinct styles, not only of thought, but of expression. Evidently its chief purpose is to depict the labor of love, or the triumphs of love, over the most untoward circumstances. The following speech of Helena beautifully illustrates the unwavering and self-confident power of this absorbing passion: —

> "Our remedies oft in ourselves do lie,
> Which we ascribe to Heaven; the fated sky
> Gives us free scope; only doth backward pull

Our slow designs, when we ourselves are dull.
What power is it which mounts my love so high,
That makes me see, and cannot feed mine eye?
The mightiest space in fortune, nature brings
To join like likes and kiss like native things.
Impossible be strange attempts to those
That weigh their pains in sense, and do suppose
What hath been cannot be. Whoever strove
To show her merit that did miss her love?"

The plot, like that of "Cymbeline," is taken from Boccaccio. With the single exception of the story of Zeneura, it is unquestionably the best in the Decameron.

The heroine, Giletta de Narbonne, is the daughter of a distinguished physician at the court of Roussilon, in France. When but a child she falls in love with a handsome youth, Count Beltram de Roussilon, with whom she was brought up. His father's death obliged him to go to Paris. Giletta was almost inconsolable during his absence, and anxiously awaited some pretext to go thither to see him. Her hand, the author tells us, was sought in marriage by many on whom her guardian would willingly have bestowed her, but she rejects them all without assigning any reason. She receives intelligence that the King is suffering from a painful and dangerous disease, which had baffled the skill of the ablest physicians of the land. She suddenly conceives the idea of going to Paris with the hope of curing him with one of her father's prescriptions. Her plans are soon put in execution. The King receives her with the utmost kindness, and promises her, if she succeeds in conquering his disease, to bestow her in marriage on a person of noble birth. Through her skill he is completely restored to health, and she claims the hand of her playmate and early love, Count Beltram de Roussilon. The Count at first rejects her offer of marriage with scorn and contempt, but finally consents to the union in obedience to the wishes of his sovereign. He deserts her upon the day of the wedding, and engages in the war of the Florentines against the Senesi.

Giletta does everything in her power to win his love and esteem, and to induce him to return to his home. Her conduct is indeed exemplary. Her subjects almost worship her for her queenly dignity, modesty, beauty, prudence, virtue, and wisdom. These excellences make no impression whatever upon her husband, who refuses to return to her only on the seemingly impossible conditions that she shall bear him a son, and obtain possession of a ring which he always wears upon his finger. Love is too deeply enthroned in her bosom to allow her to despair. She disguises herself as a pilgrim, and goes to Florence, where she learns that the Count is making improper overtures to a lady of that city. She becomes acquainted with her, and, through her, obtains possession of the ring. She also induces her to make an assignation with him, in which she supplies her place. Giletta gives birth to two sons, and the Count, on learning her stratagem, is confounded with love and admiration, and lives with her ever afterward with great joy and happiness.

The principal incidents in the story are followed with wonderful minuteness and fidelity in the drama. The poet changed the name of Giletta to Helena, and Beltram to Bertram.

Hazlitt, whose love for SHAKSPEARE is almost idolatrous, and who indeed openly confesses his idolatry, says that the poet dramatised Boccaccio's novel "with great skill and comic effects, and preserved all the beauty of the character and sentiment without improving upon it — which was impossible."

This praise is perhaps too extravagant, though it is difficult to imagine anything finer in the way of a story than

Boccaccio's, for it is told with the utmost simplicity, sweetness, and pathos. But SHAKSPEARE has, we think, improved it by elaborating the incidents, and by adorning it with new creations, and developing the individual beauty of the heroine. Indeed, it could not be otherwise. The truth is, that SHAKSPEARE'S genius consecrates everything it touches. He carries the world along with him, and whenever an object pleases him, he gives it a new life and beauty. A power mightier than Nature's seems ever to be unbosoming its secrets to him. It is impossible to describe his soft and delicate fancy, or the breadth and clearness of his vision; for he sees all things as far as angels' ken. Everything about him is subtle, wonderful, and magical. He gives even "to airy nothing a local habitation and a name." All his creations are symbols of truth and moral beauty. They address every feeling of humanity, every sentiment and passion. He bestows grace and dignity upon the most common-place subjects, and they become ever afterward objects of delight and reverence.

His female characters have an irresistible charm about them for which we may look in vain for a parallel elsewhere. His Helena is a pure effusion of genius. She is the very apotheosis of womanhood. She is not only a maid too virtuous for the contempt of empire, but the most perfect ideal of a wife. Our thoughts refer to her again and again, and each time with increasing admiration and delight. The depth and intensity of her love, and the refinement and purity of her principles, vibrate with every breeze of feeling. Her gentleness and resolution are almost equal to her beauty, and she is described as one

> "Whose beauty did astonish the survey
> Of richest eyes, whose words all ears took captive;
> Whose dear perfection hearts that scorned to serve,
> Humbly called mistress."

She is placed in the most trying situation, and surrounded by the most degrading circumstances. In her the ordinary rules of courtship are reversed. She is compelled to appear herself as a wooer, and to court her lover both as a maid and as a wife, and yet she does not violate a single law of modesty or propriety. Her combination of intellect and passion is truly wonderful. Her self-possession never deserts her. She is ever looking forward to a bright and happy future. She seems to hope even against hope, and to believe when faith seems fatuity. What could be finer than her description of her love for Bertram, who, by the laws of society, is placed above her in social position?—

> "My imagination
> Carries no favor in it but my Bertram's;
> I am undone — there is no loving, none,
> If Bertram be away. It were all one
> That I should love a b.ight particular star,
> And think to wed it, he is so above me;
> In his bright radiance and collateral light
> Must I be comforted not in his sphere?
> Th' ambition in my love thus plagues itself;
> The hind that would be mated by the lion
> Must die for love."

Poor Helena, true to the instincts of her sex, has not the slightest idea of her own merit. When she cannot win her lord to look upon her, she thinks it is because she is unworthy of him.

Her unwearied patience is rewarded at last,

> "For time will bring on summer,
> When briars shall have leaves as well as thorns,
> And be as sweet as sharp."

It has been well questioned whether Bertram deserves her unconquerable faith of affection, her deep and lasting attachment. Dr. Johnson describes him as a man noble without generosity, and young without truth. He condemns him, as well as he may, for sneaking home to a second marriage, and defending himself with falsehood against his wife's accusations. His foolish pride of birth seems to be his greatest fault. His compulsory marriage, "being compelled to submit his fancy to other eyes," when the ardor and impetuosity of his youth longed for freedom and frowned upon restraint, should, we think, in some measure, extenuate his conduct. Besides, his faults seem absolutely necessary in order to develop Helena's intensity of passion, and strength and firmness of character. It is impossible to help loving the Countess, Helena's guardian. She is a living and an essential truth. Mrs. Jameson says, "She is like one of Titian's old women, who still amid their wrinkles remind us of that soul of beauty and sensibility which must have animated them when young." She is a perfect mistress of her own thoughts. The rose of her spirit is kept bright and beautiful to the last. Age cannot dull her sensibilities, or curb even for a moment the sweet and gentle, and kind and generous, and pure and holy emotions of her soul. The purity of her principles and her self-forgetting love are enough to evoke the admiration of the angels. She is never unmindful of the lessons of experience, but ever cherishes them as sacred treasures. How beautiful are her reflections when she discovers the pangs of Helena's unrequited love! She says:—

> "Even so was it with me when I was young.
> * * * This thorn
> Doth to our rose of youth rightly belong;
> It is the show and seal of Nature's truth,
> When love's strong passion is impressed in youth."

The witty and eccentric Lord Lafeu is a very charming character.

Every one has the utmost contempt for Parolles. His

impudence and poltroonery are disgusting in the extreme. "His soul is in his clothes." He is, in every sense of the word, a contemptible "pronoun" of a man. Critics may well marvel that this "lump of counterfeit ore" "should know what he is and be what he is." "He is created on purpose for men to breathe themselves upon." He is "a notorious liar," "a great way fool," and "solely a coward;" and yet the elements of wit and humor are so mixed in him that he furnishes us with an inexhaustible vein of mirth and laughter.

DREAMING.

The subject of Dreaming is always interesting. It is too deeply interwoven with philosophy and superstition to be otherwise than interesting. Dugald Stewart defined Dreaming to be a series of thoughts not under command of reason, or that condition in which we have nearly or quite lost all volition over bodily organs, but in which those mental powers retain a partial degree of activity.

It has been said that though the power of volition does not seem to be altogether absent in sleep, the will appears to lose its influence over the faculties of the mind and members of the body, which during our waking hours are subject to its authority.

In sleep we seem to experience every kind of emotion, and at times our reasoning powers appear to be as clear as the noonday sun. Spurzheim and Gall, in their Physiognomical system, affirm, in the most positive manner, that we often reason better when dreaming than when awake. Hazlitt, however, makes a good deal of sport of this theory, and calls it a fine style of German mysticism.

It is generally supposed that dreaming is an evidence of imperfect sleep, but it is possible that the state of sleep is always accompanied by dreams, though we may not be able to remember them.

At a dinner party we heard one of the most distinguished authors in the country remark, that if he ever dreamed in his life he did not know it, and that if it were not for the positive assertions of others, he would be forced to disbelieve in dreams.

Locke relates an incident of a gentleman who never dreamed until he was twenty-six years of age, when he had a fever and dreamed for the first time.

On the authority of Plutarch, we learn that Cleon and Thrasymedes, both of whom lived to an advanced age, never experienced the phenomenon of Dreaming. Upham, in his Mental Philosophy, refuses to admit the possibility of such cases, arguing that they may have dreamed and forgotten, but adds, undoubtedly such persons dream very seldom. Kant inclines to the same opinion, and says that those who fancy they have not dreamed, have forgotten their dreams. The truth is, we know so little about Dreaming that it is almost useless to speculate on the subject.

Nearly all the ancient philosophers and moralists believed in the Divine or spiritual character of dreams. Plato believed that all dreams could be trusted when the body and mind are in a healthy condition. The sublimest illustrations, however, of the prophetic character of dreams are found in the Bible. For instance, those of Saul, Solomon, Abimelech, and Daniel, in the Old Testament, and those of the wise men of the East, of Joseph, and of the wife of Pilate, in the New Testament. The following passage from the Scriptures seems to proclaim the prophetic character of dreams:—"In slumbering upon the bed, God openeth the ears of men and sealeth their understanding."

The dream of Calphurnia the night before the assassination of her husband, Julius Cæsar, is perhaps the most extraordinary example we have in profane history of this kind of dreaming.

Columbus dreamed that a voice said to him, "God will give to thee the keys of the gates of the ocean."

The theory that dreams are but the continuation of our waking thoughts is very popular in Germany and France, and, indeed, one of the most distinguished savans of the latter country asserts that some of his most profound and abstruse calculations were left in an unfinished state, and completed in his dreams after he had went to bed. While on the subject of the relation of dreams to our waking thoughts, we will relate Coleridge's story of the composition of one of his most beautiful poems, " Kubla Khan."

In the summer of 1797, Coleridge retired to a farmhouse on the Exmoor confines of Somerset and Devonshire. He was ill, and had taken an anodyne. He fell asleep in his chair while reading the following lines in " Purchas's Pilgrimage " : —" Here the Khan Kubla commanded a palace to be built, and a stately garden thereunto, and thus ten miles of fertile ground were enclosed with a wall."

He continued to sleep very profoundly for several hours, during which he composed not less than two to three hundred lines of poetry. On waking he endeavored to write out what he had composed, but was called away on business just as he had written that part of the poem he has given us in his published works. When he returned he was unable to finish the poem ; but what he wrote ere the charm was broken contains a world of beauty.

> " In Xanadu did Kubla Khan
>   A stately pleasure-dome decree,
>   Where Alph, the sacred river, ran
>   Through caverns measureless to man,
>   Down to a sunless sea.
>   So twice five miles of fertile ground,
>   With walls and towers were girded round,
>   And there were gardens bright with sinuous rills,
>   Where blossomed many an incense-bearing tree,
>   And here were forests ancient as the hills,
>   Enfolding sunny spots of greenery. "

Coleridge then pictures a wild, romantic chasm, where huge fragments vaulted like rebounding hail, amid the tumult of which Kubla Khan heard from afar,

"Ancestral voices prophesying war."

The poem concludes with a description of a dome of pleasure, in which an Abyssinian maid sings with the sweetest symphony of Mount Abora.

> " Singing of Mount Abora.
> Could I revive within me
> Her symphony and song,
> To such a deep delight would win me,
> That with music loud and long
> I would build that dome in air;
> That sunny dome! those caves of ice!
> And all who heard should see them there,
> And all should cry, Beware! Beware!
> His flashing eyes, his floating hair;
> Weave a circle around him thrice,
> And close your eyes with holy dread,
> For he on honey-dew hath fed,
> And drunk the milk of Paradise."

One of the most singular things connected with Dreaming is the rapidity with which time seems to pass while in that state.

Dr. Carpenter relates an incident of a clergyman falling asleep in his pulpit during the singing of a psalm before the sermon, and awaking with the conviction that he must have slept for at least an hour, and that the congregation had been waiting for him, but on referring to his book he was consoled by finding that his slumber had lasted only during the singing of a single line.

The apparent reality of dreams has often occasioned many ridiculous blunders in leading persons to relate their dreams as actual occurrences. One of the most religious and truthful men we ever knew on one occasion assured us that he had traveled in Russia, when we were satisfied that he had scarcely been outside of the confines of the neighborhood in which he lived. We have also heard a distinguished professor in a leading medical college of Kentucky say that he had dreamed so much about the catacombs at Paris that it was impossible for him to tell whether he had actually visited them or not. This, however, is not so bad as the story of the man who dreamed that his head had been cut off, and refused to believe otherwise until allowed the privilege of looking at himself in the glass. However, none of these examples are any more extraordinary than a dream of our own which we will relate.

A few years ago, after a severe and continued spell of sickness, we dreamed that we had received a letter from a friend in Europe. It was written at Geneva. The scenery of the surrounding country was glowingly described. Nearly all the famous names in history with which this romantic place is associated, including those of Gibbon, De Stael, Necker, Kemble, Rousseau, and Voltaire, were recalled and commented upon with singular clearness and beauty. We had the most vivid impression of reading the letter over and over again, and of putting it in the drawer of our writing-desk, with the intention of perusing it again after breakfast. On waking the impression was not dispelled. It became for a time an actual event in life, as palpable to the senses as what we feel and touch.

We were mortified beyond endurance an hour or two afterwards, when we related the supposed fact of having received the letter to a friend, who informed us that the gentleman had not gone to Europe, but contemplated doing so in the course of a few months.

Fortunately, however, we are not often troubled with the difficulty of being unable to distinguish between our waking and sleeping thoughts, and when we are, we console ourselves with the reflection that those who never dream never think.

DANTE.

DANTE has been fortunate in his translators. Cary and Longfellow have perhaps furnished the best and truest to the spirit of the original. Either of them will give the reader a better idea of the genius of the great Florentine than Carlyle's literal prose version.

In 1867 Dr. James Parsons published the first canto of the "Divina Commedia," in which he substituted the decasyllabic quatrain for the triple rhyme of the Italian with tolerable effect, but his work is regarded in no other light than as a free translation.

Cary's translation is even better known in this country than Longfellow's. Prescott said of it:—"If DANTE could have foreseen it he would have given his translator a place in his ninth heaven."

But notwithstanding this praise, and the popularity of the work, it lacks the music, the *terza rima*, the "continuous interchanging harmony" of the original. Longfellow, in the opinion of our ablest critics, has given us a rigorous adhesion to the words and idioms of the text, and at the same time has preserved all its delicious and entrancing music. We rejoice to know that DANTE is now being more thoroughly read and studied than ever before. No poet who has ever lived has equaled him in intensity of feeling or surpassed him in fiery bursts of passionate eloquence. He has often been compared with Petrarch, but there is little or nothing in the poetry of the latter to justify the comparison. It is true that there is much to admire in Petrarch, but there is also much that is prurient, insipid, and disgusting. We weary of his love speeches to Laura. They are too monotonous. They lack strength, variety, depth, and originality. The incident he relates of seeing a young peasant girl, on a summer day, washing in a running stream a veil of the same texture as one worn by Laura, and of his trembling before her as if in the presence of Laura herself, may be very sentimental and romantic, but we hardly think it worthy of being enshrined in verse, and least of all such verse as Petrarch was capable of writing.

DANTE'S love speeches, on the contrary, are never occasioned by such ludicrous incidents. He seems to have a soul above the aggrandisement of insignificant things. His poetry is ever marked by a uniform excellence. He is at all times terribly in earnest. It is almost impossible to think of him without regretting that the age in which he lived was incapable of appreciating his rare and wondrous gifts. It seems that fortune frowned upon him from his birth. When only nine years of age he met Beatrice Portinari, to whose love and beauty he attributed the inspiration of his genius. She died in early youth, but not until she became the wife of another. It is said that she did not wholly turn a deaf ear to his vows of affection, but maintained for him the loftiest ideas of Platonic love. His disconsolate grief on being unable to secure her for his bride, won for him the affections of the beautiful Gemma Dei Donati, a descendant of a long line of powerful and warlike nobles. His marriage with her was anything else but a happy one. In the revolution of Ghian Della, he was arrayed in the ranks of the citizens against the nobility. He was elected one of the Priors of Florence, but when the opposite party came into power he was condemned to pay a fine for an alleged malversation in office. He was sentenced to be burned alive if taken within the boundaries of the Republic. Thus cruelly banished from Florence, forsaken by his friends and relatives, he became a homeless wanderer on the face of the earth. He stopped awhile in Sienna and in Bologna, and with the Ghibelline chieftian, Fazuola, on the mountains near Ubini. It is said that he wandered to France and England, and was seen in Paris and at Oxford. Wherever he went, trouble, and pain, and sorrow marked his footsteps. He has himself said :

"Through almost all parts where the Italian is spoken, a wanderer and well-nigh a beggar, I have gone, showing against my will the wound of fortune. Truly I have been a vessel without sail or rudder, driven to divers ports, estuaries and shores by that hot blast, the breath of poverty, and I have shown myself to the eyes of many who, perhaps, through some fame of me had imagined me in quite another guise, in whose view not only my person was debased, but every work of mine done or yet to do became valueless."

In the midst of his sufferings an effort was made to procure his return to Florence. Alas! that genius should so often draw upon itself the bitterest persecution. It is not the gift of the crowd. It is an original and a creative being, ever diffusing its light upon the world, yet asking none from it. It is often idolised, crowned and sceptred, clothed in purple and decked with glittering jewels, but oftener trampled under foot, and pierced by the shafts of envy and jealousy, which, like the fabled arrows of Acestes, take fire as they fly.

The conditions on which DANTE was allowed to return to Florence were conceived in a spirit of the bitterest malignity. We can form some idea of the loftiness of his pride from a letter on this subject addressed to a relative: —

"I will return," said he, "with hasty steps, if you or any other can open to me a way that shall not derogate from the fame and honor of DANTE; but if by no other way Florence can be entered, then Florence I shall never see. What! shall I not everywhere enjoy the light of the sun and the stars, and may I not seek and contemplate in every corner of the earth, under the canopy of heaven, consoling and delightful truth, without first rendering myself inglorious, nay, infamous, to the people and Republic of Florence? Bread, I hope, will not fail me."

A monument was erected to him at Ravenna, where he passed the last days of his life. Florence made two formal demands for his remains, but the city that had given him a home in his distress could not, in justice to itself, grant the request.

In person, DANTE was above the medium height. His complexion was of a dark olive. His eyes were dark and piercing, and of a singular brilliancy of expression. His countenance was resolute and determined, and ever displayed a shade of melancholy. His disposition was naturally mild and gentle, but became harsh and irascible through intense mental suffering.

By the common consent of mankind, his "Divina Commedia" ranks with the "Iliad" and "Odyssey." His Beatrice, as portrayed with her flowing hair and starry eyes, and cheeks whose roseate hue shames the glory of the morn, whose breath is the perfume of the opening rose, whose snowy bosom swells with love's own sighs, is indeed no mortal, but an angel of light, throned among the supremely blest. He was the first poet of his country who gave elegance of style and diction to his native tongue. He has been often called the father of Italian literature. The statesmen and scholars of his time thought it an evidence of vulgarity to speak or write in any other language than the Latin; but DANTE found in the speech of the illiterate peasantry the sweetest tones of music.

"Di Monarchia" and the "Convito" are, perhaps, his most popular prose works.

Mr. Norton has recently translated the "Vita Nuovo.' His version of "Il Dolarosa" is greatly admired.

Shelley's translation of the ode entitled " A Wish," which we give below, is unequaled for the exquisite flow of its numbers: —

> "Guido, I would that Lappo, thou and I,
> Led by some strong enchantment, might ascend
> A magic ship, whose charmed sails should fly
> With the winds at will, where'er our thoughts might wend,
> So that no change or any evil chance
> Should mar our joyous voyage, but it might be
> That even satiety should still enhance
> Between our hearts their strict community;
> And that the bounteous wizard then would place
> Vanna and Bice and my gentle love,
> Companions of our wanderings, and would grace
> With passionate tales, wherever we might rove,
> Our time, and each were as content and free
> As I believe that thou and I should be."

The Gypsies.

The Gypsies are wholly ignorant of their origin, and have kept but an imperfect record of their migrations; but it is evident that they are a distinct race of people. Like the Jews, they have no country of their own, and are scattered over all parts of the globe. Time has made little or no change in their peculiarities. They have the same language, personal appearance, habits, and customs, that they had centuries ago. The name of Gypsies (meaning Egyptians) is doubtless an incorrect one. At least we know of nothing to justify them in the assumption of the title. In Italy they are called "Zingari," in Germany "Zigeuner," in Spain "Gitanos," in Turkey "Tchengenler," in Persia "Sisech Hindu," in Sweden "Tartars," and in France "Bohemiens."

Borrow expresses the opinion that the name of Gypsies originated among the priests and learned men of Europe, who expected to find in Scripture some account of their origin and some clew to their skill in the occult sciences.

Simson, the author of a recent work entitled the "History of the Gypsies," believes that they are a mixture of the shepherd-kings and the native Egpytians, who formed part of the "mixed multitude" mentioned in the Biblical account of the expulsion of the Jews from Egypt. Grellman, however, traces their origin to India. He says that they belong to the Soodra caste. Vulcanius describes them simply as robbers and outlaws, and Hervas regards their language as "a mere jargon of banditti."

Their keen black eyes, swarthy complexion, long raven locks, high cheek-bones, and projecting lower jaws evidently indicate Asiatic origin. It is certain that neither their language nor physiognomy are African. It is argued that if really Egyptians, they would in all probability have preserved a religion, or some of the forms of worship so characteristic of the descendants of that people; whereas, the Gypsies have no religion at all.

Indeed, it is a proverb with them that "the Gypsy church was built of lard, and the dogs ate it."

Whether Egyptians or not, they are doubtless what they claim to be, "Rommany Chals," and not "Gorgios." Very few who have seen them will refuse to believe that they do not understand the art of making horse-shoes, and of snake-charming, fortune-telling, poisoning with the drows, and of singing such songs as the following:

"The Rommany chi
And the Rommany chal
Shall jaw tasaulor
To drab the bawlor,
And dook the gry
Of the farming rye."

"The Rommany churl
And the Rommany girl
To-morrow shall hie
To poison the sty,
And bewitch on the mead
The farmer's steed."

At one time the Gypsies were under the protection of the Scottish kings. James IV. gave Antonius Gawino, who claimed to be "Count of Little Egypt," a letter of recommendation to the King of Denmark.

It is well known that James V. issued a document guaranteeing protection to "Our lovit John Faa, Lord and Erle of Litil Egypt." This document also called upon the people of Scotland not to molest the said John Faa or his band "in doing their lawful business." It has been a matter of conjecture what that business was; but it was, doubtless, as Mr. Petelengro would say, "business of Egypt."

The history of the Faas is singularly interesting. The tribes in England and Scotland were ruled by them for several centuries.

Andro Faa possessed sufficient influence with the crown to procure a pardon for manslaughter in 1554.

In the seventeenth century one of his descendants, Captain John Faa, made such an impression on the heart of the beautiful Countess of Cassilis, that she was persuaded to elope with him from her husband, but the Captain and most of his band were soon afterward captured and executed.

This incident gave rise to the celebrated song entitled "The Gypsie Laddie." We give below the first and concluding verses: —

> "The Gypsy came to Lord Cassilis' yett,
> And O but they sang bonnie;
> They sang sae sweet and sae complete,
> That down came our fair ladie.

> "They were fifteen valiant men,
> Black, but very bonnie,
> And they all lost their lives for ane —
> The Earl of Cassilis' ladie."

The Faas afterward changed their name to Fall. Many of them were distinguished for their fine personal appearance, dignified and elegant bearing, and superior mental accomplishments. They are connected by marriage with some of the noblest families in Scotland. Captain James Fall, member of Parliament, was particularly proud of his Gypsy origin, and took every opportunity to boast of it; and a Mrs. Fall, wife of the Provost of Dunbar, represented with her own hands, in needle-work, the whole family, "with their asses and Gypsy paraphernalia, leaving Yetholm."

According to Mr. Simson, it is almost impossible to tell in Scotland who are not Gypsies. He says that they are to be met with in every sphere of Scottish life, and that he is acquainted with youths and men of middle age, of education and character, who follow very respectable occupations, who are Gypsies. He thinks that the race has become so prolific that there are probably 500,000 of them in the British isles alone.

One of the Miss Falls married Sir John Anstruther, of Elie, Bart.

It is said that during an exciting election for Parliament, in which Sir John was a candidate, that his opponent taunted him with his wife's Gypsy origin, and sought to injure him by reference to it. The streets, it is said, resounded with the song of "The Gypsy Laddie," whenever Lady Anstruther entered them, and on one occasion a friend expressed the deepest regret that the rabble should thus insult her. "Oh, never mind," replied Lady Anstruther, "they are only repeating what they hear from their parents."

The Gypsies have a great passion for horses, and treat them with the utmost kindness. It is well known that while they will eat almost every kind of carrion, they will not touch the flesh of a horse.

It would seem that there is a peculiar charm attached to Gypsy life, for it is seldom that one of their number deserts them, and when he does he is almost sure to return the first opportunity. Hence the saying: "Once a Gypsy, always a Gypsy." But there are a good many who take the appearance of Gypsies without having a Gypsy origin, and this reminds us of an amusing anecdote related by that accomplished scholar and author, Noble Butler. While riding on the top of an omnibus in the Duke of Devonshire's grounds, he saw before him a gang of what appeared to be Gypsies. A gentlemen sitting by him said, "A great many dye their faces in this part of the country, and pass themselves as Gypsies, that they may beg and steal." As the omnibus rolled on, a little boy ran out from the gang to the side of the omnibus, crying out, "Please to lave us a pinny," with unmistakable Irish accent. The Gypsy diet is said to be very savory and palatable, but while we, like Dominie Sampson, might be won over to the goodly stew of Meg Merrilies, which was composed of fowls, hares, partridges, and moor-game, boiled in a mess with potatoes, onions, and leeks, we hardly think that we could become reconciled to the doctrine that "what God kills is better than what man kills."

This curious people are superstitious in the extreme. They consult the stars, the flight of birds and the soughing of the wind for good and evil omens; and it is said they watch a corpse by day and night until it is buried, and believe that "the Diel tinkles in the lykewake" for those who feel, during what is called the "death-throe," the terrors of remorse. They are both cowardly and treacherous, and are not only malicious, but cruelly vindictive. They seem to have every vice but the want of chastity. The marriage tie with them is regarded as sacred. The ceremony of divorce is very imposing, and is performed around the body of a dead horse, sacrificed for the occasion at the time of high noon.

Both sexes have an inordinate passion for jewelry, and

have ever exhibited a fondness for a union of filth and tawdry finery. But whatever may be said of them, the virtue of their women is inviolable. It is seldom if ever conquered, and when it is, the punishment is death. We have heard of a beautiful Gypsy girl who left her camp near Madrid one evening, attracted by the strains of delicious music, to engage in the festivities of a ball-room. She was received with the utmost enthusiasm, and loaded with jewels and caresses. When the guests had departed, she was detained by one who hoped to accomplish her ruin. She, for a time, heroically resisted every attack upon her virtue, but yielded at last. The next morning she was found hung upon a post not far from the scene of her crime. The country was instantly scoured for the purpose of bringing the malefactors to justice, but there was scarcely a vestige of the camp left, nor was there a Gypsy to be seen in the neighborhood for many years afterward.

Autographs.

The collection of Autographs seems to have begun about the middle of the sixteenth century. The Germans claim that the custom first originated in their country. I know of no reason to deny them this honor; and I cheerfully accord to them the right of sharing it in common with the renown of giving to mankind the three great elements of modern civilisation — printing, gunpowder, and the Protestant religion, and of being the first to catch the light of Shakspeare's genius and to reflect it upon the world.

The custom is said to have originated among travellers, who carried with them a book or album for the purpose of securing the signatures of distinguished persons. The oldest book of this kind is dated 1558. It is in the British Museum, the repository of the most valuable collection of Autographs in the world.

Magna Charta, granted in 1215, is also deposited there. This instrument serves to establish the fact that neither the king nor any of his nobles could write their own names. The signature of Shakspeare is perhaps the most precious of all autographic treasures. Five of his autographs, known to be genuine, have been preserved. One of them is his last will and testament, and is deposited at Doctors' Commons, London. It bears his signature in three places.

A number of scholars have tried to establish the theory that the character may be determined by the rapid writing.

Their arguments, however, are entitled to but little consideration.

Hood, in one of his essays, makes a good deal of sport of a gentleman who asked him for his autograph. He pretended not to know what kind he wanted. He said autographs were of many kinds. For instance, charity boys write theirs on large pieces of paper, illuminated with engraving; Draco wrote his, to oblige Themis, in human blood, and servants sometimes have a habit of scrawling autographs on a tea-board with slopped milk. He concluded by telling the gentleman that as he had not sent him a brick wall, or a looking-glass, or a bill-stamp, or a kitchen-door, that he supposed he wanted a common pen, ink, and paper autograph; but in the absence of any particular direction for transmitting it, either by a carrier-pigeon or in a fire-balloon, &c., he would send him one in *print*. Hood was fully aware of the dignity of the profession of the genuine autographic collector, but could not resist the temptation of indulging in his quaint and inimitable humor.

The collection of Autographs, pursued in the proper spirit, cannot do otherwise than increase historical and biographical knowledge.

One of the most distinguished collectors in the United States is Mr. L. J. Cist, of St. Louis. He is not only a fine scholar, but one of the best judges of the genuineness of letters and manuscripts in the country. He was for many years a resident of Cincinnati, and is the author of a volume of delightful poems. I had heard so much of his famous collection that I felt no little curiosity to examine it and to talk with him about it. I went to St. Louis a few years ago, and had the pleasure of making his acquaintance. He received me with the utmost kindness and cordiality. The subject of Autographs was soon introduced, and in a few moments I found myself surrounded by his priceless treasures. He informed me that he began his collection more than thirty years ago. He said that he came accidentally into the possession of the signatures of three Presidents of the United States — Madison, Monroe, and John Q. Adams. These led him to wish for others. He then undertook to make a small collection of some of the most prominent living American statesmen and authors, in which he succeeded.

His collection now comprises about twelve thousand letters and documents, written or signed, of which about one-half are American, the rest European, with a small sprinkling of Asiatic and African (the King of Siam, Rammohun Roy, Hussein, the last Dey of Algiers, the Presidents of Liberia, &c., &c.), illustrated with about eight thousand engraved portraits and views, and not less than fifty thousand newspaper-cuttings containing biographical, historical and anecdotal matters of interest relating to the persons whose autographs they illustrate, classified as follows : —

AMERICAN — ANTE-REVOLUTIONARY.

Colonial and Royal Governors, Proprietaries, Judges, Statesmen, &c., before the Revolution, in which may be found the autographs of more than one hundred and fifty of the original founders, proprietors, and early Governors of the thirteen colonies from 1630 to 1776, including such names as Roger Williams, Duke of York (James I.), Lord Berkeley, Sir George Carteret, William Penn and sons, Cecil Lord Baltimore, and General Oglethorpe, founders or proprietaries. Of the Governors of Massachusetts from John Endicott, John Winthrop, and Sir Henry Vane, down to Hutchinson and Gage, the last two Royal Governors of Massachusetts, wanting only John Haynes (Governor from 1635 to

1636) to be complete. Of New York, Peter Stuyvesant (an autograph letter), Sir Edmund Andros (an autograph letter), Thomas Dongan, Jacob Leisler, Sir Charles Hardy, DeLancey, Cadwallader Colden, General Monckton, Lord Dunmore, and the last Royal Governor Tryon. Of Pennsylvania, Thomas, Richard, and John Penn, Lloyd, Markham, James Logan (from whom the famous chief was named), and others. Spottiswood, Drysdale, Dinwiddie, Fauquier, &c., of Virginia; Dobbs, Tryon, Craven, Middleton, Francis Nicholson, Reynolds, Wright, and others of North and South Carolina and Georgia.

Of Statesmen and Judges, are Chief-Justice Samuel Sewall, of Massachusetts; also the Judges who tried, and Geo. Corwin, the sheriff who hung the witches at Salem; Col. James Otis, the elder (father of the great orator and patriot), the Delancys (Oliver, Stephen, and James); leading men of New York in old Colony times, &c., &c.

Here also may be found two very rare documents of special interest to typos, the first being —

"The humble memorial of William Bradford, printer, to the Governor and Council of the Province of New York, etc., sheweth:

"That the tenth day of this instant, January, there was one quarter's salary due to him, and humbly prays that it may be allowed.

"And, further: That, whereas, he came to serve their Majesties in this government by printing such things as there might be occasion of for their Majesties' service," &c., he goes on to state that "he has printed for their said Majesties' service as much as hath stood him in £50 charge, and not sold of the same to the value of £5," &c., and therefore humbly prays their favorable consideration of the same, and subscribes himself, &c.

This rare and precious relic of the first printer of Pennsylvania and New York is unfortunately not dated, but as "their Majesties" alluded to were William and Mary, the memorial must have been written between the years 1693 (in which Bradford came to New York) and 1695, in which Queen Mary died. Bradford was born in England in 1659, came to America in 1683, and landed where Philadelphia now stands, before a house was built there.

He was the first printer there, and in 1687 published an almanac. He removed to New York city in 1693, and was for thirty years the only printer in the Province, now State of New York, and in 1725 started the *New York Gazette*, the first newspaper published there. He died May 23, 1752, at the ripe old age of ninety-three.

The other interesting typographical document of early date referred to, is a short note from James Franklin, the elder brother of Ben. Franklin, with whom the latter served his apprenticeship and learned the trade of a printer. He started in 1722, at Boston, the *New-England Courant*, which was the third newspaper ever started in America. He afterward, in 1732, published the *Rhode Island Gazette*, the first paper published in the Province of Rhode Island.

Any one familiar with the well-known chirography of Dr. Franklin, looking at this paper, will be struck by the remarkable similarity in the style of handwriting of the two brothers. Probably Benjamin, who was younger than James, was taught to write by his brother. If so, the pupil afterward far excelled his master in this as in most other acquirements.

Next we have in this division the Generals and officers of the French and Indian Colonial wars, including all the British Generals commanding-in-chief in America from 1755 to 1775, viz., Braddock, Shirley, Loudoun, Abercrombie, Amherst, and Gage, together with many Colonial officers of distinction, such as Sir William Pepperell, Sir William Johnson, Generals Dwight, Waldo, Winslow, Col. Ephraim Williams, and others.

Two other series belonging to Colonial times and history are the Delegates to the Convention which met at Albany in 1754, and the members of the Colonial (or Stamp Act) Congress of 1765, the former consisting of twenty-five delegates from New Hampshire, Massachusetts, Rhode Island, Connecticut, New York, Pennsylvania, and Maryland; the latter of twenty-seven members, representatives of the Colonies of Massachusetts, Connecticut, Rhode Island, New York, New Jersey, Pennsylvania, Delaware, and South Carolina. Each of these series in this collection lacks but two names of being full and complete.

The earliest American paper in the collection is an autograph of Governor John Winthrop, of Massachusetts, bearing date "(3) 23 — 40;"— March 23d, 1640. A document signed by Thomas Dudley, Governor in 1645, is the only other American specimen of earlier date than 1650. There are some eighteen or twenty written between 1650 and 1685, between which latter date and the close of the seventeenth century the specimens are numerous.

The reader's attention is now invited to another part of the collection, if possible still more interesting. It is the department devoted to the autographs of distinguished men during what may be called the Revolutionary period, from 1774 to 1788. It opens at once to the student a world of thought and reflection. It embraces the prominent Generals and Statesmen not only of the Revolution from 1775 to 1783, but up to the time of the Constitution of 1787, when the Confederation gave way to the more vigorous form of our present government. This department includes the following subdivision: —

THE SIGNERS OF THE DECLARATION OF INDEPENDENCE.

It contains one or more original letters of every one of the signers of that instrument. Some of these letters are of the deepest interest, as, for example, where Josiah Bartlett, of

New Hampshire, writes, under date of January 29th, 1775: "This colony chose deputies who met in congress at Exeter the 17th day of May last, and agreed to raise two thousand men for the common defense of the colonies;" or where William Whipple, in September, 1776, says:—"It seems to be settled that our troops have quitted Long Island. The consequence there will be that they must also evacuate New York;" or where John Adams writes Elbridge Gerry, from Paris, 1780:—"What am I to do for money? Not one line have I received from Congress or any member of Congress since I left America." There is also a letter from William Williams, dated May 25th, 1775, to the "Delegates from Connecticut to ye General Congress," with a reply to the same, signed by Eliphalet Dyer and Roger Sherman, relating to the capture of Ticonderoga. The answer of William Floyd, dated July 4th, 1821, to the address of his fellow-citizens who had met to celebrate the anniversary of Independence, is of special interest when we think that he was then in his 87th year, and that he died August 4th, 1821, precisely one month afterward.

Here is found a letter from Dr. Franklin, written in 1750, inclosing a draft of a course of study "for the English School," in which he says:—"I am very unfit, having neither been educated myself (except as a tradesman) nor concerned in the education of others." Another letter of Franklin to his wife, dated London, July 5th, 1769, is characteristic for the style of its address, commencing, "My dear child," and ending, "Your affectionate husband, B. Franklin."

Here are letters of Robert Morris, the great financier of the Revolution, some written when he filled the office of Secretary of Finance, and others penned in jail, where he died a prisoner for debt. One member of the Pennsylvania delegation, writing to his wife in 1776, concludes with, "I am in good health and spirits, and live mostly at my own little house, as the people call it. Give Peggy, Betsy and Jim each a buss for me. I write this in Congress chamber, not having time to go to my lodging, and am, dear Ellen, your loving and affectionate spouse, James Smith. Mr. Hancock [meaning John Hancock] calls me to the other room. Adieu. J. S."

A long letter from William Hooper details the landing of the enemy, in 1781, at Wilmington, and the capture of his family and property there, saying:—"Where I shall go from this, God knows. The world is open before me. Without a family and without property, I bear my all about me."

Francis Lightfoot Lee, writing to his brother, Richard Henry Lee, in 1777, from Yorktown, says:—"I have received no letters from Richmond these two posts past. There is some rascality in the postoffice. I wish you could find it out." Postmasters, even in those early days, were not always immaculate.

We have a letter from John Hancock (1778) to Dr. Franklin in Paris, one from John Adams (1779) to Arthur Lee, and Robert Truit Paine (1778) to Elbridge Gerry, Roger Sherman (1781) to Josiah Bartlett, Francis Lewis (1778) to Governor George S. Clinton, Charles Carroll to General Washington, Thomas Jefferson (1779) to Richard Henry Lee, Richard Henry Lee (August, 1776) to Patrick Henry, and Thos. Nelson to B. Harrison.

Here I saw an autograph of Thomas Lynch, Jr., cut from the fly-leaf of a book, the only one extant save his signature to the original document at Washington. His letters have been sought for in vain by collectors in South Carolina and elsewhere.

Forty-eight autographs of this department are what are

called holographs, letters or documents entirely written and signed by the writers.

A large majority of the signers of this instrument had passed from the stage of action more than a generation before Mr. C. began his collection. It will be seen that his task was one of the utmost difficulty. He accomplished it in about fifteen years. His success in its final completion is equaled only by the energy and patience he brought to bear upon it.

I regret that I have time only to notice briefly that part of Mr. Cist's collection comprising the distinguished Generals and officers of the Revolutionary war. He has in this department about three hundred and fifty original letters, including letters from Washington, Kosciusko, DeKalb, Lee, Wayne, Marion, Sumter, Pickens, and others. This branch of his collection is illustrated by two hundred engraved portraits. It also includes letters from a number of distinguished British officers, such as Burgoyne, Howe, and Cornwallis. There is also a letter from the famous Indian chief, Joseph Brandt, or Thaendaneger, written in 1795, in which he expresses, in very good English, his indignation at the Indians being compared to the French. "Indians," he says, "are not wholly destitute of humanity."

There is another division which comprises the Presidents and members of the old (or Continental) Congress from 1774 to 1778. This interesting series contains autographs of all the Presidents (fourteen in number), and about three hundred of the three hundred and fifty Revolutionary worthies who represented their States (the old thirteen) in Congress during the fifteen years above mentioned. The Presidents were Peyton Randolph, Henry Middleton (acting for a few days only), John Hancock, Henry Laurens, John Jay, Sam'l Huntington, Thomas McKean, John Hanson, Elias Boudinot, Thomas Mifflin, Richard Henry Lee, Nathaniel Gorham, Arthur St. Clair, and Cyrus Griffin.

Next after the Continental Congresses comes the Annapolis Convention of 1786, the precursor of the Federal Convention of 1787, which formed the present Constitution of the United States.

This Convention, called by the Congress, consisted of the following delegates from their respective States:— Alex. Hamilton, and Egbert Benson, New York; Abraham Clark, Wm. C. Houston, and James Schureman, New Jersey; Tench Coxe, Penna.; John Dickinson, George Read, and Richard Bassett, Delaware; James Madison, Edmund Randolph, and St. George Tucker, Virginia. It met Sept. 11th, 1786, chose John Dickinson as its chairman, and adjourned Sept. 14th, having limited its labors to the recommendation of a more general convention from all the States, to be held in Philadelphia the following year.

That Convention, which met in May, 1787, is generally known as the "Federal Convention of 1787," and its members are designated by autograph collectors as the "Signers" or "Framers of the Constitution of the United States."

The number of Delegates who *attended* the Convention, and took part in its proceedings, who may be called the "Framers of the Constitution," was 55, of whom, however, only 37 (including Geo. Washington as President, and Wm. Jackson as Secretary), were actually *Signers* of the instrument when completed. Besides the 55 delegates in attendance, there were 10 others (65 in all) originally appointed, but who declined, or failed to attend the Convention. It will be seen it is thus a difficult matter, in making a list or collection of the autographs of the "Members of the Federal Convention" or "Signers of the Constitution," to decide of how many and what names it shall be composed. Some collectors confine themselves to the Signers proper, others collect all the members who actually attended the Convention. Mr. C. having, many years ago, completed both these, subsequently extended his plan to embrace *all* those who were *elected* or *appointed* delegates to the Convention, whether they attended it or not, and his series now consists of choice letters of every such delegate, with but a single exception.

The balance of the collection, which may be classified under the general head of

LITERARY, SCIENTIFIC, AND MISCELLANEOUS,

is further sub-divided into

AUTHORS.— Historians and Biographers, Novelists and Belles-Lettrists, Poets, &c.

SCIENTIFIC. — Naturalists, Inventors, Travellers, and Arctic Voyagers, &c., &c.

MEDICAL, CLERICAL. — From Increase and Cotton Mather down, including complete a series of the Bishops of the Protestant Episcopal Church since the commencement; another (nearly complete) of the Methodist Bishops in the United States, from Coke and Asbury down; together with all the Archbishops, and most of the eminent Bishops of the Catholic Church, from its first American Bishop, John Carroll, to the present day.

MISCELLANEOUS. — Distinguished Jurists, Judges, and Lawyers; Editors and Politicians; Hartford Convention, &c., &c.; while a curious miscellaneous medley brings up the rear, in which the names of Lafitte the Pirate, Burr and Blennerhassett, Walker, Lopez and other filibusters; Davy Crockett, Lorenzo Dow, and Lord Timothy Dexter; the Rapps, Robert Owen, and Fanny Wright; Joe Smith and Brigham Young; Siamese Twins, Barnum, and Tom

Thumb; John Ross, the Cherokee Chief, Wm. Lloyd Garrison; and John Brown, whose

> "Body lies mouldering in the grave,
> While his soul is marching on"—

all jostle each other, or like

> "Black spirits and white,
> Blue spirits and gray,
> Mingle, mingle, mingle,
> Those that mingle may."

JANAUSCHEK.

It is somewhat singular that we should find among the Germans the greatest delineator of one of the sublimest of Shakspeare's characters. We have always had the highest appreciation of German intellect. We thought that they knew more about everything else than about the art of acting. We knew well enough that they had taught us something about the arts and sciences, about criticism, mechanism, aesthetics, poetry, philosophy, and religion ; but until we saw JANAUSCHEK, we could not divest ourselves of the idea that they are awkward and clumsy.

Schlegel had but an indifferent opinion of German acting. He said that the theatre was at a very low ebb. He did not attribute this deficiency to a want of talent among his people for dramatic art, but to a want of proper appreciation and cultivation of it. In speaking of German plays he says, "there is too much romance in them," and that "the word romantic is too often profaned by being lavished upon rude and monstrous abortions."

If the Germans, generally, have not produced great actors, they have certainly produced some of the greatest critics upon Shakspeare, if indeed they were not the first to catch the light of his genius and reflect it upon the world. Hazlitt, in speaking of German criticism, says, " I am free to confess that my national pride was wounded at the reflection that it was reserved for foreign critics to give reasons for the faith that the English have in Shakspeare." Hazlitt's admiration for Schlegel was unbounded. He said that " no one has shown the same enthusiastic admiration for Shakspeare's genius, or the same philosophical acuteness in pointing out his characteristic excellence."

These compliments to Schlegel are richly deserved, for his criticisms will compare favorably with those of any of the English critics. Lessing, we believe, was the earliest, if not indeed the greatest of the German Shakspearean scholars. But Herder in the "Blätter von Deutscher Art," and Kunst and Tieck in "Letters on Shakspeare," and Goethe in "Wilhelm Meister," and Schiller and Schelling, are other august examples of the German appreciation of Shakspeare's genius. Our indebtedness to German criticism will be more fully appreciated when we recollect how unfavorably Shakspeare has been treated by some of the ablest English scholars and authors. For instance, Dr. Johnson sneers at him, and says that his pathos is not natural, but far-fetched and full of affectation, and that his characters are mere "species, instead of individuals." Hume, the historian, also vents his spleen against him who is the first in the world's literature, and in the appreciation of the arts, sciences, religions, knowledge, and philosophy; who has conjured up landscapes of immortal fragrance and freshness and beauty, and peopled them with beings who have displayed all the varied and complicated phases of humanity, and whose thoughts, speeches, words, sentiments, passions, and imaginings, have become the common property of mankind. Hume says, "It is in vain that we look into Shakspeare for either purity or simplicity of diction. His total ignorance of all theatrical art and conduct, however material a defect, yet, as it affects the spectator rather than the reader, we can more easily excuse than that want of taste which prevails in his productions."

Whether or not we acknowledge the supremacy of German criticism in regard to Shakspeare, we must acknowledge the grandeur, power, and beauty, and pathos of JANAUSCHEK's acting in Lady Macbeth, which is, perhaps, the least understood of any of Shakspeare's characters.

Lady Macbeth is generally regarded as a mere bloodthirsty and despicable female fury, but JANAUSCHEK has given us an insight into those sweet and tender and gentle emotions of the soul which made the Thane of Cawdor regard and address her as the dearest partner of his greatness.

Some years ago we spoke of JANAUSCHEK in connection with Ristori, but there is really no comparison between them. Ristori may have strength, power, beauty, and originality of conception, but she lacks the culture, the refinement, the intellect, the delicacy of feeling, the profound thought and depth of penetration, the subtle and keen analysis of character, the wonderfully varied emotions and passions, the energy, the spirit, the fire and genius of her rival.

We have said that there is no comparison to be made between these two great artists, but we are reminded that both of them lend their splendid gifts to the delineation of such sensational dramas as Giacometta's "Elizabeth." This abominable play has been translated into the French, the German, the Spanish, and the English languages, and has been made popular in this country by the acting of Mrs. Lander, Ristori, and JANAUSCHEK. It abounds in ridiculous and sensational passages, and presents little or no claims to either dramatic art or literary merit. There is one scene in the third act which strikes us as particularly objectionable. It is where Elizabeth is dictating two letters at once, one to the Earl of Leicester and the other to Chief-Justice Popham. She is represented as delivering her words in an arrogant and imperial tone, and at the conclusion she pronounces her name Elizabeth with startling effect. The strangest part about it is that this scene is always vehemently applauded — but perhaps, after all, not so strange as that a gifted and highly cultivated artist should abuse her talents in thus attempting to display such clap-trap nonsense. Elizabeth, though endowed with more than the usual vanity of her sex, attached her name, in all probability, to public documents, letters, and State papers, with very little parade, at least without indulging in such unnecessary bombast and pomposity.

But to return to Lady Macbeth. A short time since JANAUSCHEK personated this character at the Boston Theatre. She was supported by Edwin Booth as Macbeth. The occasion of two such brilliant stars appearing together was indeed a rare one.. It was looked upon as an epoch in the history of the American stage. More than four thousand persons were present. The audience extended to the distant and almost suburban amphitheatre of that magnificent building. Poets, authors, scholars, orators, and statesmen were among the vast auditory that assembled to witness the performance. The acting that followed revealed beauties in Shakspeare almost undreamed of before. Booth's Hamlet was no longer considered his greatest character. The ablest critics in Boston were forced to acknowledge that, if his Hamlet was the most refined and natural creation, his Macbeth was the most vigorous and brilliant.

Booth never perhaps played so well before, unless we except his acting on the occasion of the production of Macbeth for the first time at his new theatre in New York.

Such a spell of enchantment was thrown around the play, that even the weird sisters appeared not as fanciful creations but as fearful realities.

The scene previous to Duncan's murder was grandly portrayed. We felt that Lady Macbeth indeed shamed her husband with a superhuman audacity when JANAUSCHEK delivered the following:—

> "What beast was it, then,
> That made you break the enterprise to me?
> When you durst do it, then you were a man;
> And, to be more than what you were, you would
> Be so much more than man. Nor time, nor place,
> Did then adhere, and yet you would make both:
> They have made themselves, and that their fitness now
> Does unmake you. I have given suck and knew
> How tender 'tis to love the babe that milks me:
> I would, while it was smiling in my face,
> Have plucked my nipple from his boneless gums,
> And dashed the brains out, had I so sworn
> As you have done to this!"

It is said that Mrs. Siddons, in her personation of Lady Macbeth, uttered these horrible words in a demoniacal scream, as if frightened to madness by the audacity of her language. Upon which Hudson says, "We can easily conceive how a spasmodic action of fear might lend her the appearance of superhuman or inhuman boldness. At all events, it should be observed that Lady Macbeth's energy and intensity of purpose overbears the feelings of the woman, and that some of her words are spoken more as suiting the former than as springing from the latter; and her convulsive struggle of feeling against that overbearing violence of purpose might well be expressed by a scream."

When JANAUSCHEK uttered this speech, her voice suddenly assumed a deep and husky tone. There was something almost unearthly about it. Her words seemed to come from her lips shivering with horror, conveying the loftiest ideas of impassioned scorn — infinitely, we think, more effective than any maniacal scream, and which might well overcome Macbeth's determination "to proceed no further in this business."

It would, however, be a difficult matter to determine which scene was the greater: the one which we have endeavored to describe, or that in which the following dialogue takes place: —

> "*Lady M.* Give him tending—
> He brings great news.
> The raven himself is hoarse,
> That croaks the fatal entrance of Duncan
> Under my battlements. Come, all you spirits
> That tend on mortal thoughts, unsex me here;
> And fill me, from the crown to the toe, top-full
> Of direst cruelty! make thick my blood;
> Stop up th' access and passage to remorse;
> That no compunctious visitings of nature
> Shake my fell purpose; nor keep pace between
> The effect, and it! Come to my woman's breasts,
> And take my milk for gall, you murdering ministers,
> Wherever in your sightless substances
> You wait on nature's mischief! Come, thick night,
> And pall thee in the dunnest smoke of hell!
> That my keen knife see not the wound it makes,
> Nor Heaven peep through the blanket of the dark,
> To cry, 'Hold, hold!'—
>
> *Enter* MACBETH.
>
> "Great Glamis! worthy Cawdor!
> Greater than both, by the all-hail hereafter!
> Thy letters have transported me beyond
> This ignorant present, and I feel now
> The future in the instant.
>   *Macb.* My dearest love,
> Duncan comes here to-night.
>   *Lady M.* And when goes hence?
>   *Macb.* To-morrow — as he purposes.
>   *Lady M.* Oh, never
> Shall sun that morrow see!
> Your face, my Thane, is as a book, where men

> May read strange matters.—To beguile the time,
> Look like the time; bear welcome in your eye,
> Your hand your tongue; look like the innocent flower,
> But be the serpent under it. He that's coming
> Must be provided for: and you shall put
> This night's great business into my dispatch;
> Which shall to all our days and nights to come
> Give solely sovereign sway and masterdom."

JANAUSCHEK's genius is probably better displayed in the sleep-walking scene than in any other in the play. Booth himself remarked to us that this scene could not be surpassed, and that JANAUSCHEK was the only actress he ever saw who seemed capable of comprehending the lofty heroism, and womanly refinement combined with the unscrupulous daring and demoniacal fury and firmness of the character.

Her form seemed wasted with torturing and sleepless midnight watchings, and the glazed glamour displayed terribly upon her haggard countenance the ever-burning fever of remorse, when she, "open-eyed yet sightless," endeavored to free her hands from the imaginary spots of blood, and exclaimed,

> "Out, damned spot! out, I say!—One; Two; Why, then, 'tis time to do't!—Hell is murky!—Fie, my lord, fie! a soldier, and afeard? What need we fear who knows it, when none can call our power to account?—Yet who would have thought the old man to have had so much blood in him?"

She repeats the words "Hell is murky" with compressed lips, and their horrible mockery is indeed enough to sicken the soul.

This scene formed a striking contrast to the one where she endeavored to relieve Macbeth of "thick-coming fancies," when she says —

> "How now, my lord? why do you keep alone,
> Of sorriest fancies your companions making,—

> Using those thoughts, which should indeed have died
> With them they think on? Things without remedy
> Should be without regard: what's done is done."

Or in the scene where she says —

> "Come on,
> Gentle my lord, sleek o'er your rugged looks,
> Be bright and jovial amongst your guests to-night."

JANAUSCHEK does her utmost to portray the tender sympathy ever springing up between Lady Macbeth and her unhappy husband.

How different from the portraiture of Mrs. Kemble, who can see but little in Lady Macbeth's character save blood, the feeling of blood, the sight of blood, and the smell of blood, thus divesting her of those womanly touches of nature so apparent when Macbeth leans upon her for support, and says —

> "O, full of scorpions is my mind, dear wife!"

and when she tells him —

> "You lack the season of all natures, sleep."

But we have not space to dwell further upon JANAUSCHEK's acting. It is sufficient to say that her Lady Macbeth is such a creation of genius that the students of Shakspeare will be grateful for the insight she has given them into the soul of that terrible being, who was the prop and stay of "Bellona's bridegroom;" that doomed and dauntless spirit who would not "play false," and yet would "wrongly win."

A Philological Study.

Pol.—What do you read, my lord?
Ham.—Words, words, words.

The rules which form the grammar of any particular language, so far as they differ from those of any other, are occasioned by accidental and temporary circumstances. Probably for this reason these rules have been treated by our ablest scholars and authors under the head of the history of language rather than the science of language. Sir John Stoddard says that in order to understand the English grammar we must have a knowledge of universal grammar as well as of the history of language. He says that universal grammar disregards that which is peculiar to the speech of this or that individual tribe, race, or nation, and considers only what is common to man in all ages and countries, both as to an arrangement of his thoughts and feelings with a view to their communication to others, and also as to the bodily organs or instruments with which the Almighty has furnished us for the purpose of such communications.

His work on "Glossology, or the Historical Relations of Languages," dwells at length on the possibility and probability of forming from the existing languages a universal language. His investigations into the science and philosophy of language are learned and varied in the extreme. They are, however, of too speculative a character to be of much assistance to those who wish to understand the practical principles of Philology.

The English language is wholly free from that labyrinth of cases, moods, and tenses, common to the Greek and Latin.

There are but few terminations in its verbs, and none at all in its adjectives, save for the expression of the degrees of comparison. There is no language better suited for the formation of derivatives from their roots. It has none of the untranslatable idiomatic expressions of the French, the German, the Spanish, and the Italian.

One of its chief beauties is its distinction of gender, or the modification of its nouns to denote the distinction of sex through gender.

The French, for instance, have no neuter gender. Their two articles, masculine *le*, and feminine *la*, one or the other is prefixed to their substantive nouns to denote their gender, and as a natural consequence the most perplexing difficulties must inevitably follow. *Beau* in their language is of the masculine gender, and yet the fair sex are called *le beau sexe*. Vossius says that gender is properly a distinction of sex, but it is improperly attributed to those things which have not sex, and only follow the nature of things having sex in so far as the agreement of substantive with adjective. Sex is properly expressed in reference to male and female, as Pythagoras and Theona; *ager*, a field, therefore, is improperly called masculine, and *herba*, an herb, is improperly called feminine. But animal is neuter, because it is construed neither way. It never occurred to Vossius that all substantives could be properly classed by gender. Harris says that every substantive is male or female, or both male and female, or neither one nor the other, so that with respect to sexes and their negation, all substantives conceivable are comprehended under this fourfold consideration.

Harris failed to include the common gender in his classification of substantive nouns. Lindley Murray says that there is no such gender, and that the business of parsing can be done without it. Goold Brown agrees with Murray, and says the term "common gender" is applicable to the learned languages, but in the English it is plainly a solecism. Noble Butler has completely overthrown this theory. According to Butler, nouns which are applied to living beings without reference to sex are of the common gender, as parent, cousin, child, sheep, friend, neighbor. The term common gender is a grammatical term, applied merely to the words, and does not imply any common sex.

We have also what is called the transfer of gender in our own language, and by means of it we are enabled to distinguish between prose and poetry, or between the language of reality and imagination.

For instance, we can give form, distinctness, and beauty to an object by raising that object to the dignity of a person. There are some very fine illustrations of what is meant by the transfer of gender in Milton and in the Bible, though it is well enough to remark that the neuter possessive pronouns were then not generally in use.

If gender were permanently fixed in our language, the following description of thunder, in Milton, would lose half its beauty:—

"The thunder,
Winged with red lightning and impetuous rage,
Perhaps has spent his shafts."

We give below a quotation from Milton in which gender is applied with singular force and beauty to the idea of form:—

"His form had yet not lost
All her original brightness, nor appeared
Less than archangel ruined."

But perhaps the finest example that can be given of the transfer of gender occurs in a description of night in the Book of Wisdom : — " While all things were in quiet silence, and that night was in the midst of her swift course, Thine Almighty word leaped down from Heaven out of Thy royal throne, like a fierce man of war into a land of destruction."

There is a great disposition on the part of a certain class of philologists to do away with the use of the words sung and sprung.

Richard Savage has been charged with ignorance for the use of sprung and sung, instead of sprang and sang, in the lines,

" From liberty each noble science sprung —
A Bacon brightened and a Spenser sung."

But we do not know of any reason why sprung and sung should not be considered correct words. Worcester, in his large lexicon, says that *sprang* and *sang* are obsolescents, and Webster admits them partially so.

Dr. Bullion, Hallock, Pinneo, Brown, Kirkham, and, best of all, Noble Butler, prefer sung and sprung to sang and sprang. In Butler's list of irregular verbs in which the past tense and the auxiliary perfect participle are alike in form, we have :—Imperfect, or present infinitive, sing ; past indicative, sung ; auxiliary perfect participle, sung. The word sang is placed at the right of the column of past indicatives to indicate that sung is the choicest word, and the one most in use. Shone is thus placed before shined.

We have in the same list :—Imperfect, or present infinite, spring ; past, sprung ; auxiliary perfect, sprung. So likewise string, strung, strung, and swing, swung, swung. Some grammarians prefer *drank* to *drunk* for the participle of *drink*. At one time *drank* was used occasionally by good writers, but according to Mr. Butler it is only employed by writers of an inferior class. The best authors say "Toasts" were *drunk*, and not "Toasts" were *drank*. We have a correct use of the word in Coleridge's lines,

> "He on honey dew hath fed
> And *drunk* the milk of Paradise."

The following examples have been furnished me by Mr. Butler from the advanced proof-sheets of his new gramma :

"Nobody can write the life of a man but those who have ate, and *drunk*, and lived in social intercourse with him."—*Dr. Johnson.*

"The toast is *drunk* with a good deal of cheering."—*Dickens.*

"Claret equal to the best which is *drunk* in London."—*Macaulay.*

"O'Doherty's health being *drunk*."—*Prof. Wilson.*

"The health of King James was *drunk* with loud acclamations."—*Macaulay.*

"He had *drunk* largely."—*Thackeray.*

"Wine was more generally *drunk* than now."—*Hawthorne.*

"I have not *drunk* a glass of wine for twelve months."—*Hood.*

Probably enough examples have been given to show that *drunk* is preferred to drank by our best writers.

Goold Brown, Pinneo, and some other grammarians, set down bear, *to carry*, and bear, *to bring forth*, as two distinct verbs, the former with the participle *borne*, and the latter with the participle *born*. These authors are supported in their theory by Dr. Webster, who says that "a very useful distinction is observed by good authors, who in the sense of produced or brought forth write this word *born*, but in the sense of carried write it *borne*." It is true enough that in the sense of *carried* the participle is *borne*; but surely in the sense of *produced* the participle is not *born*.

We do not say the tree has born fruit, but the tree has *borne* fruit ; nor that the mother has *born* children, but *borne* children. Born is never used in the active voice, and never in the passive when followed by the preposition *by.*

It is somewhat singular that there should be any trouble whatever about the correct use of irregular verbs, and yet how often the transitive verbs *lay, raise,* and *set,* are confounded with the intransitive verbs *lie, rise,* and *sit.*

Set, set, set, and *sit, sat, sat,* are as simple as simplicity itself. We set a thing in its place, and we sit down when we are tired. The same simplicity is characteristic of lay, laid, laid, and lie, lay, lain; and yet Lord Byron, in one of the sublimest passages in *Childe Harold,* in speaking of man and his Creator, says:—

> " And sendst him shivering in the playful spray,
> And howling to his gods, where haply lies
> His petty hope in some near port or bay,
> And dashest him again to earth; there let him lay."

Such errors as "he *laid* down," for he *lay* down, are very common in conversation, but the best plan we have seen to avoid them is given by Mr. Butler. It consists simply of a table where the transitive verbs *lay* and *set* are conjugated by the side of the intransitive verbs *lie* and *sit.*

Dr. Webster contends that the phrase *you was* is correct but we fear few good writers agree with him. If *you was* is correct, it would be little use to argue that a verb should agree with its subject in number and person.

Webster says, "The verb must follow its nominative. If that denotes unity, so does the verb." But there is not much unity in a pronoun of a second person requiring the verb of the third person.

Pinneo, in his grammar, says:— " In common conversation, and by the practised class, *was* in the singular is almost always used, and among the the more highly educated the tendency is increasing daily." Mr. Butler, in commenting upon this, observes:— " If any unfortunate pupil should be led by this statement to the use of *you was,* he would soon find himself suffering the penalty of misplaced confidence."

Some persons seem to have great difficulty in seeing the difference between signification and form. No one contends that *you* always denotes more than one, as no one contends that *we* always denotes more than one, or that the German *sie* always refers to several persons spoken of. The question is simply about form.

If *you* is not always plural in form, let us say *you art;* even if we should follow the analogy of *you was* and say *you is.* And, according to the same principle, let the editor of the newspaper when he means only himself say *we am,* or *we is.* We shall then have everything, as Tony Lumpkins's friend expresses it, in "a concatenation accordingly."

The use of the plural *we* for *I* is comparatively of recent date. There certainly can be no objection to it, for it is nothing like as egotistical as the latter form. A recent writer tells us that it originated with King John, who found out the art of multiplying himself, whereas his predecessors had been content with the simple *ego*. The use of *we* by editors when a single person is meant, is explained on the ground that the opinions expressed under this form are those of a class or party. This expression, however, has the same excuse as that of *you* for *thou*. It is republican in form and respectful in every sense, and avoids direct personality.

FINIS.

A WONDERFUL BOOK.
JUST PUBLISHED.

"SEEN AND HEARD," by MORRISON HEADY, the "*Blind Bard of Kentucky,*" as he was called by the late George D. Prentice. A collection of poems by an author Blind and Deaf, would be of the highest interest, if its merits were only ordinary; but, as the work is one of *true poetry*, showing the writer to be a man of rarest endowments and high poetic genius, the "surprise and admiration" of the veteran poet Whittier cannot be wondered at, and his assertion that he "knows of nothing in modern literature more remarkable" than this book, will be reëchoed by every person that reads it. The late Geo. D. Prentice, himself a distinguished poet and a world-renowned Journalist and critic, adds new strength to Mr. Whittier's endorsement, by saying "the people of Mr. Heady's State have a right to be proud of him. When I consider the disadvantages that have doubly rested upon him throughout nearly all his life, I cannot but wonder at what he has been able to achieve."

The volume is an elegant one, beautifully printed on the *finest* tinted paper, and richly bound in a novel style — an elegant ornament alike for the Parlor Table or the Library Shelf. Price $2.00. Sent *Postage Free*, upon receipt of price to any part of the country.

H. C. TURNBULL, JR.,
54 Lexington st.,
BALTIMORE.

[*Copy of a letter written to Morrison Heady, by the late Geo. D. Prentice.*]

LOUISVILLE, KY., *Nov.* 11*th*, 1869.

MR. MORRISON HEADY,

Dear Sir:—Permit me to thank you very heartily for your recently published volume of poetry. I have read the whole of it with much pleasure, and a large portion of it with high admiration. It has passages that I think *sublime*. That such a book could be produced by a poet under the extraordinary disadvantages that rest upon you is to me a matter of wonder. Accept my best wishes for your happiness and fame.   Yours truly,

GEO. D. PRENTICE.

[*Copy of a letter received by the publisher from the late Geo. D. Prentice.*]

LOUISVILLE, *Nov.* 17*th*, 1869.

MR. HENRY C. TURNBULL, JR.,

Dear Sir:—I thank you for a very finely printed and bound volume of the poems of Morrison Heady, the Deaf and Blind poet of Kentucky; I think that it has very fine merit. I have known the Author many years, and always regarded him as a man of genius and true inspiration. The people of his State have a right to be proud of him. When I consider the disadvantages that have doubly rested upon him throughout nearly all his life, I cannot but wonder at what he has been able to achieve.

Very respectfully,
GEO. D PRENTICE.

[*Copy of a letter received by the publisher from the celebrated and veteran Poet,* J. G. WHITTIER]

AMESBURY, 13th *October,* 1869.

DEAR SIR:

I thank thee for a copy of the beautiful volume of my friend Heady's Poems. Some years ago I read with surprise and admiration the opening poem in the book, in which he described with almost Miltonic power and pathos his *double night* of blindness and deafness. I have looked over the long Indian Poem, which, notwithstanding what seems to me an unfortunate rhythmical method, is full of felicitous passages of description and characterisation, which any one in possession of all his senses might well be proud of. The same might be said of the *Apocalypse of the Seasons,* which rises from quiet pastoral beauty to a lofty hymn of Christian faith and hope. As might be expected, the volume is open to criticism, *but I know of nothing in modern literature more remarkable than its production under the circumstances in which its author is placed.*

I am, very truly, thy friend,
JOHN G. WHITTIER.

COPY.

[*Extracts from a letter, published in the* "Virginia Gazette," *written by* MRS. MARGARET J. PRESTON, *author of* "Beechenbrook," *and other poems.*]

Nothing superior to the volume *Seen and Heard,* in typography, paper or binding, has ever been issued from any press south of Philadelphia. * * * * The Poems *Seen and Heard* ought not to be arraigned at the bar of ordinary criticism. The knowledge that they are the production of one who is forever shut within that drear domain,

"Where echoless *Silence* tolls the passing bell—
Where shadowless *Darkness* weaves the shrouding spell,"

as he himself so mournfully describes it in the Poem entitled *The Double Night,* would, or at least *should*, drain from the bitterest critical pen all its venom. And even were the contents of the book far less creditable than they are, who would not stretch out in utmost tenderness, a helping and pitying hand to aid the uncertain footsteps of this sad groper through Olympian arcades?

MR. HEADY's pages abound in such rich imagery, display so much delicate sketching from nature, and manifest an almost Flemish finish in details, that it is hard to persuade oneself that almost since childhood he has been wrapped in "ever-during dark." But Providence has given him a compensation in the possession of

"That inner eye,
Which is the bliss of solitude."

* * * * Heartily do we commend this volume to the kind appreciation of the reading public. We feel sure that the blind man's exquisite sense of touch must be gratified as he passes his hand over

the creamy leaves and handles the rich binding. We hope for him the still higher gratification of a wide circle of most appreciative readers.

Seen and Heard. Poems or the like. Why Mr. Heady allowed the last three words of the title to accompany the other four, we cannot understand; for if his be not poetry, we know not what is: and poetry, too, of a high order. * * * * * The longest poem in the book is YOONEMSKOTA : *an Indian Idyll.* It enters as fully into Indian modes of thought and feeling, and speech, as Longfellow's *Hiawatha*, and is, in our opinion, fully equal to it in everything except perhaps the artistic finish. Nor is it an imitation: for, in the first place, it is written in several different measures; and in the second place, parts of it date back to 1852. which is three or four years earlier than the publication of *Hiawatha.* * * * In the *Apocalypse of the Seasons,* at the close of the book, the description of that apparently unpoetical thing — the Reaping Machine — is equal to anything in Thomson. We wish we had space for it; but we must content ourselves with advising our agricultural friends to get the book and read it for themselves. * * * The book is beautifully gotten up, and will bear comparison with the best productions of the American Press.—*Southern Review.*

* * * *Yoonemskota* follows the *Double Night,* and is full of many beauties, and written in that style so very rare and beautiful, seldom found, and strange to say, by the " mass " of readers, not appreciated as its truly beautiful rhythm merits. * * * *The End of Time* is an unparalleled poem, which, in awful sublimity and grandeur, exceeds anything we have ever read. * * * This collection of poems, taken separately or collectively, is a rare jewel, and should grace the library of every lover of what is really beautiful. * * * The volume is gotten up in the very best style, surpassing in fact anything we have ever seen.—*Spencer Journal,* Ky.

* * * It is interesting to note what perceptions he still retains from the days when he looked out on the world with youthful eye, not knowing how brief the time allotted him to amass a treasure of fair sights and sounds to serve as his portion of earth's beauty during his life-time to come. It is interesting to note these memories, their vividness, and the skill with which he uses the things which he *has* once " seen and heard." * * * * We are astonished at the wealth of a memory which is ever ready with life-like pictures, as if the poet had come fresh from the hills and forests of his native Kentucky, to fix the fleeting images on paper.

Yoonemskota, an Indian Idyll, is decidedly the most powerful and original of these poems, both in matter and in form. * * * * The descriptions of scenery in the poem are everywhere singularly fresh and vivid. For instance, the moon-rise, where we actually see the widening light, the sharp edge suddenly protruding above the peak, and then the full-orbed splendor as the planet disengages herself and hangs clear and round in the sky. So the sunset and the sunrise, with the successive awakening of motion and life among inanimate things, the creatures of the forest, and finally the red men in their lodges. * * * But Mr. Heady can depict sweet and peaceful scenes as well as savage ferocities, and depicts them too in befittingly musical verse. * * * We feel no hesitation in pronouncing Mr. Heady a poet of *true genius* and no mean skill in his art, whose works under any circumstances would attract notice and deserve praise; but which, considering the deprivations under which the author suffers, are little less than wonderful. We should not do entire justice to the book were we to omit to notice the extreme elegance of its dress and general finish, on which the publisher seems to have spared neither care nor cost.—*Baltimore Statesman.*

iv

* * * "*Seen and Heard*," is the title of an elegant volume of poems, * * * all of which display poetic power, and even if not issued under peculiar circumstances, which lend additional interest, the work would be worth while as one of the best collections of amateur poetry made for some time. The elegance of the paper, typography and binding, are worthy of note.—*New York Evening Mail.*

* * * Mr. Heady's compositions show a great deal of poetical feeling, and profound sensibility to and love of the phenomena of nature, and they are ethically of a transparent purity and sweetness. It is impossible to say how high Mr. Heady would have risen in his chosen path with the use of all his exterior senses. For one deprived of the two chief ones, his powers of imagination, expression and description are very remarkable, and the poetical merit of his compositions *very high*.—*American Publisher and Bookseller*, N. Y.

This strangely named volume is the product of a *true* and *remarkable* genius. Deprived of sight and hearing when a youth, whatever imagery the poet draws of external nature must come from memory's storehouse, lighted up by fancy's glowing lamp. Hence, "Seen and Heard." And it is surprising how well stored is his memory, and how vividly the poet's fancy paints the many-voiced and ever-varying outer world that has so long been to him as a sealed book. His shorter poems are smooth of verse, pathetic, finely expressive in language and versification. In "Yoouemskota" Mr. Heady shows himself to be a poet of original and varied powers. Here we have the Indians, and their haunts, and their ways of life, the seasons and their phenomena, all the varying aspects of nature, limned with rare freshness, force and fidelity, *aglow* with striking and *highly* poetical imagery, and evincing no common mastery of rhythmical harmony and variety of movement. There are scenes or situations in this poem so *uncommonly fresh and vivid* in conception and handling, as would furnish *worthy* subjects for the *greatest living Painters*. * * * Mr. Heady is certainly no "mute, inglorious Milton." Only one of a very rare order of endowments could have written these poems under similar afflictions. The style in which the volume is brought out reflects high credit upon the publisher.—*New Orleans Picayune.*

* * * These poems exhibit a power of personification equal to that of Shelley, and a delicacy and truthfulness of touch in word-painting that imparts to their descriptions of nature a life-likeness, reminding us of Keats' *Eve of St. Agnes*. * * * * * *The Apocalypse of the Seasons* is a poem that we were charmed with at first sight, and have learned to love more and more with each successive reading, until admiration has become a passion. * * * The book is appropriately named. For although the poet is blind and deaf, so *real* are his conceptions that we are constrained to acknowledge he has *seen* deeper into nature's soul, and heard more of her confidential whispers than ourselves, with eyes and ears open to every sight and sound. He has almost beguiled us of our sympathy for his affliction, and tempted us to covet a glimpse of the glorious worlds of fancy " forever *singing* as they shine," which has made his "Double Night," "a day supernal."—*Baltimore Episcopal Methodist.*

* * * Mr. Heady's privations, which in ordinary men would be regarded as a sufficient reason for inactivity, seem to have stimulated our author to preternatural thirst for knowledge and industry in its acquisition. The result we have in part in the exquisite volume now before us. The art of the printer has fitly set these jewels. No one need fear to purchase lest he should buy pinchbeck for gold, or paste for diamonds. * * * Those loving true poetry will buy the volume and read for themselves. The enjoyment we guarantee.—*Lexington Gazette.*

www.ingramcontent.com/pod-product-compliance
Lightning Source LLC
Chambersburg PA
CBHW020307170426
43202CB00008B/529